THE UNIVERSITY OF KENTUCKY

THE MATURING YEARS

THE UNIVERSITY OF KENTUCKY

THE MATURING YEARS

BY CHARLES GANO TALBERT

1965 · LEXINGTON, KENTUCKY

UNIVERSITY OF KENTUCKY PRESS

378.76
T 14

TO BEN JARETT TALBERT

PREFACE

THE CENTENNIAL of the University of Kentucky is an appropriate time for a critical look at the past as a guide to the future. The first hundred years of the institution's history have been colored by the attitudes of many Kentuckians, but none more so than the students and faculty who without reserve have dedicated their lives to building a university of substance in spite of inauspicious origins and early years.

Throughout the nineteenth century and well into the twentieth, many Kentuckians looked upon higher education as a private matter. If a man could afford to send his children to college, he would, presumably, do so. If he could not, the loss to the state was recognized by few. This attitude had killed Kentucky's first public university, Transylvania, which after degenerating to the level of a secondary school was sold in 1865 to a religious denomination. But in the same year a new beginning was made. Under the terms of the Morrill Act of 1862, a school of agriculture and the mechanic arts was established in Lexington as one of the colleges of a denominational school called Kentucky University. This strange union could not have been expected to last. In 1878 the public school began its separate existence as the Agricultural and Mechanical College of Kentucky. Four years later it moved across town to the campus which, as the University of Kentucky, it still occupies.

Some of the religious denominations in the state looked upon the Agricultural and Mechanical College as a dangerous rival to sectarian education. In the Kentucky legislature they tried to destroy its financial support, and they came close to succeeding. That the school survived was due in large measure to the tenacity of one man, James

Kennedy Patterson, its President. When Patterson retired in 1910, the continuation of the school was assured. Its character, however, would be shaped by those who would serve it in the years to come. This history covers these formative years at the University of Kentucky under the administrations of three of its presidents, Henry S. Barker, Frank L. McVey, and Herman L. Donovan.

Source materials for a history of the University of Kentucky are voluminous. Upon his retirement in 1937 the institution's longtime registrar, Ezra L Gillis, began the task of creating the University Archives. With the assistance of Miss Mary Hester Cooper, who has continued the work since the death of Mr. Gillis, the papers of the Presidents and of many of the professors have been collected. College and departmental files are available, as are files of the school's catalogues, yearbooks, and student newspapers. Minutes of the meetings of all governing and policy-making bodies, the Board of Trustees, the University Senate, the University Council, and the University Faculty have been preserved. Of inestimable value has been the twenty-three volume, manuscript diary of President McVey, presented to the University by his children. All of these sources have been consulted, together with the files of the Lexington *Leader,* the Lexington *Herald,* and the Louisville *Courier-Journal,* and all have contributed to this history.

Aid and encouragement have been given by many persons. Dr. Herman L. Donovan, Dr. Thomas D. Clark, Dr. Harold H. Downing, and Dr. John S. Chambers have furnished information gained in the course of their long association with this institution. Dr. Clark, in particular, has been helpful in evaluating source materials. Dr. James F. Hopkins' history, *The University of Kentucky: Origins and Early Years,* is indispensable to an understanding of the institution up through the Patterson administration.

The booklet, *The University of Kentucky: Its History and Development, 1862-1955,* prepared by Ezra L Gillis, is a compendium of useful data.

Valuable editorial work has been done by Dr. Elisabeth S. Peck of Berea College. Acknowledgment should also be made to Mildred Luckey and William Patrick Monaghan, who served as research assistants, and to Kitty Frazier and Elaine Satchwill, who typed the manuscript.

Northern Community College   C. G. T.
University of Kentucky

CONTENTS

PREFACE   PAGE vii

I. THE PATTERSON HERITAGE   1

II. SIX YEARS OF STUDENT LIFE   11

III. SERVING THE COMMONWEALTH   24

IV. SIXTY-NINE RECOMMENDATIONS   35

V. A NEW PRESIDENT   48

VI. NEW COLLEGES AND DEPARTMENTS   66

VII. DEPTHS OF THE DEPRESSION   81

VIII. HOLDING THE LINE   101

IX. BRICKS AND MORTAR   115

X. MORE CHANGES   123

XI. THE WAR YEARS   137

XII. KEEPING THE UNIVERSITY FREE   152

XIII. THE POSTWAR YEARS   160

XIV. COMPLETING THE PATTERN   178

INDEX   199

ILLUSTRATIONS

HENRY STITES BARKER   FACING PAGE 2

FRANK LE ROND MC VEY   FACING PAGE 50

HERMAN LEE DONOVAN   FACING PAGE 146

CHAPTER I

THE PATTERSON HERITAGE

WITH the retirement of James K. Patterson, the University of Kentucky entered a new era. By his firm guidance Patterson had brought the Agricultural and Mechanical College through years of trial and had seen it transformed into the beginning of a true university. Largely by his own force he had preserved the school and had won for it a measure of the public support which a state institution needs to flourish. He had gathered a faculty which shared his devotion to the school, he had laid out its organization into a university, and he had placed upon it the impress of his personality. Now he handed this establishment over to a new president. To Henry Stites Barker, a former judge of the Kentucky Court of Appeals but a man of limited background both in education and in administrative experience, who assumed his new office in January, 1911, would fall the task of leading toward maturity the institution which Patterson had formed.

State University, Lexington, Kentucky, as the school was called when Judge Barker took it over, consisted of seven colleges each under the direction of a dean. These were the College of Agriculture under Dean Melville A. Scovell, who served also as Director of the Agricultural Experiment Station, the College of Mechanical and Electrical Engineering under Dean F. Paul Anderson, the College of Arts and Science under Dean Arthur M. Miller, the College of Mining Engineering under Dean Charles J. Norwood, the College of Civil Engineering under Dean Walter E. Rowe, the College of Law under Dean William T. Lafferty, and the Teachers College under Dean Louis

F. Snow. There was also at the time an Academy designed for the further preparation of students not yet qualified for college work; the principal of this was Walter K. Patterson, brother of the President Emeritus. Governing the University was a Board of Trustees made up of eighteen members. The Governor of the state, the President of the University, and the Superintendent of Public Instruction were ex officio members. The other fifteen members were appointed by the Governor for six-year terms staggered in such a way that the terms of five members expired at the end of every two years. One of the fifteen was James K. Patterson, President Emeritus, who had made membership on the board a condition of his retirement.

Internal and purely academic matters were controlled by the President with the assistance of a Vice President, a Council, the Faculty, and the Assembly. The Vice President at this time was James G. White, who had served as acting President for almost a year between the resignation of Patterson and the arrival of Barker. The Council, which was an advisory board to the President, consisted of the Vice President, the deans of the colleges, and the Dean of Women. The Faculty was composed of the Council, the President Emeritus, the registrar, the military commandant, the directors of Physical Education, and all professors and associate professors. This body formulated rules pertaining to entrance requirements, courses of study, and discipline, and also made recommendations to the Board of Trustees regarding degrees to be granted. The Assembly, consisting of all officers and the entire teaching staff, might be called by the President to consider any question relative to the general welfare of the University.

In 1911 the campus of State University, located on the south side of Lexington, contained 52 acres of land. There

HENRY STITES BARKER

was also an Experiment Station Farm of 243 acres situated about three-quarters of a mile southeast of the campus; in addition to the usual barns and outbuildings, it had a two-story brick residence, and here Dean Scovell lived. Near the main campus were Patterson Hall on the north, a residence for women students, and the Experiment Station Building on the south. Both faced Limestone Street. On the campus proper some fifteen buildings were located, all of brick trimmed with stone or terra cotta.

The Administration Building, containing offices, a chapel, and recitation rooms, was located at the approximate center of the campus. North of it stood the Gymnasium, which became the present Armory. Its one-story right wing was a drill hall. Its two-story left wing contained the gymnasium proper on its upper level, and a swimming pool, baths, and lockers for men below. The three-story center portion housed offices, an armory, the YMCA Hall, the Alumni Hall, three literary society halls, the Trustees' Room, and lockers for women.

The Education Building (now Frazee Hall) near the northwest corner of the campus housed the School of Home Economics as well as the Teachers College, shortly to become the School of Education. The Old Experiment Station Building south of the Administration Building had become the home of the School of Chemistry. Soon it became known as the Old Chemistry Building and finally housed the Infirmary and the Department of Hygiene and Public Health. Located at the southeast corner of the campus, the New Chemistry Building was the left wing of the larger building now known as Kastle Hall. Agricultural Hall, at the southwest corner of the campus, was designed to be one wing of a much larger building, but the proposed addition was never constructed. One dormitory for men was located northeast of the Administration Building, and another, slightly newer, southeast of the Old Chemistry Building. Years later these two buildings were converted to classroom use and became known as White Hall and Neville Hall.

The three Engineering Colleges occupied three and one-half buildings. Mechanical Hall with its connecting shops stood near the newer of the men's dormitories. It was the home of the College of Mechanical and Electrical Engineering. North of the New Chemistry Building was the large Civil Engineering and Physics Building (now Pence Hall). Near this were the two Mining Engineering Buildings, one for classroom work and the other for laboratory use. An observatory, equipped with an 8-inch telescope, stood between the New Chemistry Building and Mechanical Hall. Behind the Old Chemistry Building was Science Hall (now Miller Hall), which provided room for the College of Law on its third floor. Behind the Administration Building was the Library, which houses the Museum of Anthropology, built with funds donated by Andrew Carnegie, a small structure, but adequate for a university that owned no more than twenty thousand volumes at that time, thirteen thousand of which were not kept in the main library, but at the Experiment Station or in college or departmental libraries.

The new President soon became acquainted with one of the problems that face the administrator of a university. The death of Melville A. Scovell, who had been Dean of the College of Agriculture and Director of the Agricultural Experiment Station, left a distressing gap in the college that was closest to Judge Barker's heart. Dr. Joseph H. Kastle, a chemist who had returned to the Experiment Station a year earlier after several years of teaching at Johns Hopkins and at the University of Virginia, was named to fill the vacancy. After four years as Dean and Director, Kastle, too, died. The places of such men as Scovell and Kastle were very hard to fill. Another death which created a problem was that of James G. White. He had taught mathematics in the University for thirty-five years and, at the time of his death, was Dean of Men, as well as Vice President of the University. A comparative newcomer with a doctorate from Cornell, Paul P. Boyd, was appointed to the position in mathematics, while C. R. Melcher, professor of French and German, received the appointment of Dean of Men. The office of Vice President was left vacant.

One accomplishment during the early years of Barker's presidency was the creation of a Graduate School with the appointment of Alexander St. Clair Mackenzie as Graduate Dean. Though the University had been granting the master's degree for many years, the administration of graduate work had not been formally organized. Four years later, Mackenzie resigned to accept the presidency of another college. For the next eight years the Graduate School was without a dean, and a committee supervised the work of postgraduate students.

In the spring of 1911 further reorganization of the University took place. The Teachers College became at this time the School of Education and was placed in the College of Arts and Science. The Academy was to be replaced by a Model High School, which the School of Education was to conduct; unfortunately several years elapsed before the Model High School was in full operation. One casualty of this change was the principal of the Academy, Walter K. Patterson, who had held the post for many years. Also planned by the Executive Committee of the Board of Trustees were changes in the colleges of engineering. The College of Civil Engineering and the College of Mechanical and Electrical Engineering were to be merged into a College of Engineering with F. Paul Anderson as Dean. At the same time the College of Mining Engineering would become the College of Mines and Metallurgy. Of the changes in engineering, only the latter was effected. The civil engineers objected strongly to the merger, and action by the entire Board of Trustees reversed the Executive Committee and the question was not raised again for five years, though it would ultimately have a fatal effect upon Judge Barker's administration.[1]

Numerous changes were also made in the status of various related courses of study. For example, the College of Arts and Science now consisted of a School of Arts made up of the Departments of English, Mathematics, History, Latin, Greek, Modern Languages, and Philosophy; a School of Science, which included the Departments of Anatomy and Physiology, Geology, Physics, and Zoology; a School of Chemistry, which had sufficient strength to resist being classed as a mere department; and a School of Education. The College of Agriculture now had its School of Agriculture, including the Departments of Agronomy, Animal Husbandry, Bacteriology, Entomology, Horticulture and Botany, and Soil Physics; a School of Home Economics; a School of Extension; and the Experiment Station, which had its various divisions. The College of Mechanical and Electrical Engineering and the College of Civil Engineering each consisted of two schools, and the College of Mines and Metallurgy had three schools. The College of Law, however, was not divided into either schools or departments. Physical Education for Men, Physical Education for Women, and Military Science were not placed in any college, being classed as general University departments.

The faculty remained about the same as President Patterson had left it. Many taught in two fields or held

[1] Minutes of Board of Trustees, April 12, December 12, 1912; Minutes of Executive Committee, October 26, 1912, July 29, 1913; Minutes of Council, October 9, 1916; Minutes of Faculty, June 1, 1912; *Catalogues,* 1912-1913, 1914-1915, 1916-1917; *The Idea,* September 18, 1913; Lexington *Herald,* October 17, 1913.

administrative posts in addition to their teaching duties. Only six of the faculty held the Ph.D. degree; three had the M.D., and one had an M.S. from Oxford and was a Fellow of the Royal Society of Literature. Three of the Ph.D.'s were in the School of Chemistry—Franklin E. Tuttle, Ralph N. Maxson, and Lloyd C. Daniels. The other three were Dean Scovell, Glanville Terrell, who taught Greek and philosophy, and James Edward Tuthill, who taught history and political economy.

Henry Stites Barker had assumed the presidency of State University under several disabilities. Handicapped by limited education and by lack of experience in either teaching or educational administration, he also felt often-times balked by the presence on the campus of his predecessor. In his new role of President Emeritus, Patterson not only continued to live in the President's House, which he had occupied since 1882, but he also remained a member of both the Faculty and the Board of Trustees.

When Judge Barker had been mentioned as a presidential possibility, Patterson had expressed strong opposition. While the two men had been friends, Patterson thought that Barker did not measure up to the standard he had outlined to the board for use in choosing a successor. One of the more influential board members, however, remarked that as a member of the board Judge Barker had always accepted Patterson's recommendations without questions and, as President, would likely continue to look to his predecessor for guidance.[2] Thus Patterson, though relieved of routine tasks, would continue to make the policy for the institution. Such a future would naturally appeal to an administrator who at seventy-seven years of age might find it difficult to change his habits.

[2] Minutes of Board of Trustees, December 13, 1910, May 30, 1911; Minutes of Executive Committee, October 23, November 21, 1911, April 12, 1912; Lexington *Leader*, July 9, 1911; Patterson notes in Patterson Papers; "Testimony Taken by Special Investigating Committee," II, 50.

The new administration began with both men present on the campus, each of them assuming that he would have the last word in running the University. Unfortunately their views on how to manage the school differed greatly. During his long tenure Patterson had attended personally to all kinds of things, from handling institutional business and directing the repair of buildings to conferences with students about their schedules. On the other hand, Judge Barker believed in delegating authority—something that Patterson had never learned to do. The increase of University enrollment would have made this delegation of authority necessary in any event, but Patterson never seemed to understand this.

The two men differed also in their ideas of the services which the institution should render. Back in 1869 Patterson had accepted the position of head of a college which, according to the Morrill Act, was to offer training in branches of learning related to agriculture and the mechanic arts, without excluding other scientific studies or the classical subjects. Patterson, however, had placed classical studies and nonmechanic sciences in central positions of the school's curriculum. To agriculture and the mechanic arts he rendered little more than lip service. On the other hand, Judge Barker soon made known his intention to build up the College of Agriculture. He firmly believed that if the University could clearly demonstrate its valuable and practical service to the rural regions dominating the legislature, that body would appropriate sufficient funds for its adequate support.

The new status of Patterson as President Emeritus put him in a good position for taking an active hand in the affairs of the University. The retirement terms which he had drafted and which the Board of Trustees had accepted left him so strongly intrenched in University organizations that his actions seemed to him more like logical participation than like meddling.

Within a few months after Barker had taken office, the friendly feeling between Patterson and him had disappeared. Barker no doubt felt restive under the President Emeritus's continued presence and influence on the campus, while Patterson himself had probably been persuaded against his better judgment to accede to the selection of Barker as President of the University. A conflict therefore arose between the two men resulting in part from a misapprehension on both sides of the role Patterson was to play in the conduct of the University and in part from their differing conceptions of the aims of the University. Barker questioned some of the points in Patterson's agreement with the Board of Trustees on his retirement; Patterson retorted by questioning the legality of some of Barker's actions. In criticizing Barker before a legislative committee, Patterson remarked at one point, "A real university and not simply a big overgrown high school is what Kentucky needs today."[3]

At a called meeting in April, 1912, the Board of Trustees considered the matter of Patterson's pension and other clauses in his terms of retirement which left him with more power than a President Emeritus should have. Presently a compromise was reached. The terms presented by the compromise committee were that Patterson was to continue receiving his pension and to go on occupying the President's House, for which he had been paying and would continue to pay a rental of $20 per month. On the other hand he was to give up his official connection with the University, resign his positions on the Board of Trustees, on the Faculty, and on the library committee, surrender his office in the library, and sever all connections

[3] "Testimony Taken by Special Investigating Committee," I, 176-80, II, 54-55; Kentucky *House Journal*, 1912, pp. 2032-35; Kentucky *Senate Journal*, 1912, pp. 1288, 1567; Lexington *Leader*, January 23, February 1, 8, March 2, 1912; *The Idea*, January 23, 1912; Patterson to Editor of Lexington *Herald*, undated, and clipping from *Herald*, both in Patterson Papers; Ezra Gillis, notes in Barker Papers.

with the library. He was to pledge himself not to criticize the present administration publicly, to be absolutely neutral, and even to assist the administration. This report was accepted by the board, with Barker and two other members not voting, and with three members being absent, including Patterson. The Executive Committee of the board on the same day agreed to pay Patterson all money due him on his retirement allowance when he had complied with the above terms.

Patterson refused to accept the new conditions. Barker countered by reading the full text of the original retirement agreement between the board and Patterson, and for a second time asked that the agreement be canceled. With Patterson not voting, Barker's resolution was passed by a vote of 9 to 2. Some of the alumni took up Patterson's cause, saying that it was a shame for the University to break its contract with him. Patterson did not yield completely. Not only did he continue to live on the campus, as the board's decision permitted him to do, but he also considered himself still a trustee of the University, attending most of the meetings of the board and voting on nearly every issue.[4]

This was State University as Judge Barker found it at the beginning of his tenure. He had before him a well-developed organization, with the buildings and the faculty for future growth. But the stalemate between him and the President Emeritus was prophetic of what was to come.

4 Minutes of Board of Trustees, April 12, June 4, August 5, 1912, June 4, December 9, 1913, June 2, December 8, 1914, June 9, December 14, 1915, May 30, 1916, January 31, 1917; Minutes of Executive Committee, April 12, 1912; Alumni petitions filed with Patterson Papers; 10 pp. typescript in Patterson Papers; "Argument of Ex-President James K. Patterson Before the Board of Trustees of the State University, August 5, 1912," (Lexington, 1912), *passim*.

CHAPTER II

SIX YEARS OF STUDENT LIFE

THE students and their education were of great concern
to President Barker. In his first address to the students he
told them that he wished to be their brotherly counselor
and to help in any way that he could. He did not want
even those in vocational agriculture to be narrowly educated. For he felt that much of the loneliness of farm life
might be reduced by a broad education and that the best
way to reach the farmers was through their children.

Though he had been rebuffed in his moves against Patterson, Barker saw other changes made in the University.
One of the chief of these was the establishment in the
summer of 1913 of a School of Journalism in the College
of Arts and Science. At Barker's urging, Enoch Grehan,
city editor of the Lexington *Herald,* had gone to New
York to study the operation of the Pulitzer School of
Journalism at Columbia University. In the fall of 1914
Grehan left his position with the *Herald* to become head
of journalism studies on the campus. In addition to giving
instruction, the new school would also handle all printing
—at a considerable saving to the University. Beginning
this same fall the University shifted from an academic year
of three terms to one of two semesters. Another minor
change was the revision of the awkward name which had
been adopted in 1908 when the institution had become
a university. By an act of the General Assembly "State
University, Lexington, Kentucky" became the "University
of Kentucky."[1]

The major sports at the University when Barker came
were football and baseball. The latter, however, soon

declined in popularity, and basketball gradually took its place. The basketball season in that day did not start until after the Christmas holidays. In the seven years from 1911 to 1917 the University's basketball teams compiled a record of 56 wins and 28 losses, having winning seasons every year except 1917, when the team lost 6 games, 4 of them to Tennessee. Football during Barker's administration likewise enjoyed a series of prosperous seasons. University teams won a total of 35 games against 11 losses and 3 ties. Perhaps the high point of this sport occurred in 1914 in a game with Earlham College when Captain Jim Park personally scored five touchdowns and passed for five more —a record that still stands.

Then, as today, athletic successes were sometimes tarnished by other incidents. During October, 1912, the University had been accused of playing ineligible men in football games. Shortly afterward, on the night of October 30, a fire destroyed books, records, and furniture in the office of Dean F. Paul Anderson. At first it was believed to have been caused by defective wiring, but an investigation revealed that it had been set. Many students were questioned, and finally a former student admitted his guilt. Several years after the incident, two men who had been students at the time of the fire expressed the opinion that it had been set to destroy the scholastic records of athletes which had been stored in Dean Anderson's office.

There were times when victories in athletic contests touched off celebrations which annoyed the townspeople. On October 25, 1913, when a visiting football team had been beaten by a score of 27 to 7, several hundred students paraded through the streets of Lexington, tearing down

<hr />

1 Minutes of Board of Trustees, June 2, 1914, June 9, 1915; Minutes of Executive Committee, July 17, 1913; Minutes of Faculty, February 10, 1914; Rufus L. Weaver to Henry S. Barker, May 26, 1911, and Barker to Weaver, June 7, 1911, Barker Papers; Lexington *Leader,* August 31, September 14, 1913, June 14, 1915.

signs, taking over two beer wagons, and stopping streetcars. Two boys were seized by police for disorderly conduct. Additional policemen were called out, but they were greatly outnumbered and could do little. About ten-thirty when enthusiasm was beginning to wane, Judge Barker, Lyman Chalkley, and other faculty members persuaded the boys to return to their rooms.

Through local newspapers Barker characteristically defended the students, saying that the police had been unnecessarily harsh when the boys were guilty of nothing more than boyish pranks. He told the people of Lexington that they could not have a great university without submitting to some inconveniences. "The university without college spirit," he added, "is dead . . . and a dead university is of no value to the community in which it exists." The city commissioners and a grand jury reached the conclusion that the police were wrong and that the students were not greatly at fault.

In January, 1912, between the football and the basketball season, the University students held a meeting and passed a resolution in which they pledged themselves to do all in their power to suppress violence and rudeness at the intercollegiate games and to exert their influence to promote a spirit of good fellowship between the University and its sister institutions of learning. But it was no easy matter to bury the hatchet.[2]

Social organizations on the campus during Barker's administration included nine fraternities and five sororities. They existed, according to the school newspaper,

[2] Lexington *Leader*, December 7, 1912, January 14, 31, October 26, November 11, 1913; *The Idea*, November 7, 1912, May 8, 1913, March 11, 1915; Minutes of Board of Trustees, December 12, 1912, June 4, December 9, 1913; Diary of Frank L. McVey, August 26, 1948; E. R. Sweetland to Henry S. Barker, January 15, 1913, Barker Papers. Athletic statistics have been obtained from newspapers and from pamphlets prepared by Ken Kuhn and published by the University of Kentucky Athletics Association.

"with the idea of bringing together those who seek closer friendship and association than is found in an unorganized group, to stimulate better and more earnest work among students, and to cultivate to a certain extent the social side of college life." Freshmen and sophomore girls were not allowed to live in sorority houses, and juniors and seniors might do so only with the permission of the Dean of Women. The Pan-Hellenic Council worked with the faculty and the Board of Trustees in enforcing rules and in preventing any member fraternity from engaging in conduct which would damage the reputation of all.

A few honorary and professional fraternities had established chapters at the University. Before Judge Barker became President, Tau Beta Pi, honorary engineering fraternity, had installed its Kentucky Alpha Chapter and the Kentucky Mining Society had been formed. In Barker's first year, Psi Delta Phi, professional law fraternity, came to the campus, and student branches of the American Society of Mechanical Engineers and of the American Institute of Electrical Engineers were formed. Also in 1911 a request came from the alumni that a chapter of Phi Beta Kappa and of Sigma Xi be sought. The faculty was favorable, but these proposed societies were not obtained for many years.

In 1912 a local agricultural society became affiliated with Alpha Zeta, national honorary fraternity in agriculture, and in 1913 the honorary debating and oratorical fraternity, Tau Kappa Alpha, was installed. In 1914 the Henry Clay Law Society became affiliated with Phi Alpha Delta, national professional legal fraternity. In the same year the national advertising fraternity, Alpha Delta Sigma, formed a chapter, and Dean Mackenzie was the national president for a time.

Literary societies on the campus offered diversion and

practice to students with an interest in debating, declamation, and oratory. Winners in individual societies competed against each other, and teams were selected to meet teams from other colleges and universities. For men there were the Union Literary Society and the Patterson Literary Society, both with a long and distinguished past. For women students there was the Philosophian Literary Society, which had existed since 1882. In the School of Education both men and women might belong to the Horace Mann Literary Society. Besides the literary societies there were several other more specialized groups—the White Mathematics Club, the History Club, the Political Economy Club, the English Club, the Biology Club, the Literary Club, and the Canterbury Club for those interested in creative writing. Beginning in the fall of 1912 a YMCA secretary had an office on the campus and some of the students joined this organization. Although there was yet no music department, there was a glee club, an orchestra, and a band.

The University received considerable publicity from its dramatic organization, the Strollers. Besides playing in Lexington theaters, these students often gave performances in other towns over the state. Among their productions in the Barker period were "Brown of Harvard," "The Virginian," "Lost Paradise," "The College Widow," "Charley's Aunt," and "Father and the Boys."

In 1913 the faculty passed a resolution to the effect that the Turkey Trot, Drag, or any other such unconventional dance should not be permitted at University social functions. Dances were usually held in the Buell Armory and were sponsored by classes or campus organizations. One such group was an engineering club known as Tau Beta Kake, a name which was a parody on the honorary engineering fraternity Tau Beta Pi. The Tau Beta Kakes were not distinguished for high standing as engineering students, but they probably did not let that chill their enjoyment of college days.[3]

The time of the student at the University was not limited to study and social activities. A lyceum course featured over the years such speakers as Frank Dixon and Champ Clark, and on the campus William Jennings Bryan, John Fox, Jr., and other figures of the time addressed the students.

By 1916 seven publications originated on the University of Kentucky campus. *The Kentucky Law Journal* was published each month by the students in that college. They endeavored to make it "both a college paper and a legal journal worthy of the members of the profession in all parts of the State." It soon began to carry articles by prominent lawyers and judges both in Kentucky and in other states. One of its editors, Virgil Chapman, served in later years as United States representative and senator. *The Kentucky Kernel* was published every Thursday by members of the student body, and *The Transit* was issued monthly by students in the College of Civil Engineering. *The University Bulletin,* published by the Department of Journalism, was issued weekly "for the purpose of giving to the students, faculty, and friends of the University notice of all meetings, lectures, and entertainments upon the campus or in the city which are of general interest to the students and the university community." *The Experiment Station Bulletin Publications* made the results of

3 *The Idea,* April 27, 1911, May 9, November 7, 1912, April 3, May 8, 20, 1913, March 5, April 2, 16, 1914; February 4, March 11, 1915; *The Kentucky Kernel,* October 7, 1915, February 17, 1916; Lexington *Leader,* January 8, 18, 21, 28, February 9, 12, March 5, 17, 25, 26, May 23, 1911, March 19, 21, 28, November 8, 1912, February 6, May 25, 1913, May 17, 1914, November 10, 1915; Louisville *Courier-Journal,* January 15, 1911; *Catalogue,* 1916-1917; Minutes of Board of Trustees, December 12, 1912, June 4, 1913; Minutes of Faculty, March 3, May 19, 1911, February 7, 1913, February 6, 1914.

agricultural research available to the public. *The Kentucky High School Quarterly* was published four times a year by the Department of Education. Most of its space was given to articles which would be of interest and value to teachers in the high schools of the state. *The Kentuckian* was the University's yearbook.

One indication of the change that came with the new administration was President Barker's encouragement of a system for some self-government by the students. At the beginning of the second academic year of his administration he presented a plan to the student body in chapel. According to this plan there would be a student council, democratically elected, which would pass judgment upon cases involving cheating in class and other forms of dishonesty. He added that "the honor pledge would be required on examinations, and there would be no professor to exercise surveillance over the students."

A faculty committee was appointed to study the question, and in December, 1911, it presented a plan to the students. This was accepted by a vote of 368 to 183. It made all students members of a Student Government Organization. Its purposes were "to create a sentiment against all forms of dishonesty," and "to report to the Executive Committee [of the organization] all dishonorable conduct of any student in the institution."

The governing body or executive committee would consist of a president, a vice president, a secretary, three members from the senior class, three from the junior class, and two each from the sophomore and freshman classes. One member from each class would be a girl. Once elected to the executive committee, a student, if he proved satisfactory, would remain a member for the duration of his undergraduate career.

With the exception of cases involving cheating in class, men accused of dishonorable conduct were to be tried by the male members of the committee and women were to be tried by female members. A two-thirds vote was required to convict. If a student believed that he had not received a fair trial, he might have a rehearing before a jury of twelve students. Anyone convicted of cheating on a test or an examination would receive a sealed letter from the executive committee asking him to leave the University within a week or in less time if the committee thought it best. The committee would set appropriate punishment for conviction of other types of offenses.

The faculty approved the constitution of the Student Government Organization, though not all of its members were in complete sympathy with the plan. At the end of the first full year of the student government President Barker praised it highly. In 1913 the students modified their system of penalties to provide for a one-month suspension for a first cheating conviction and expulsion for a second offense. In 1914 a student introduced a motion to the effect that student government, or the honor system as it was usually termed, had been a failure and should be abolished. This motion was defeated by a large majority. In 1915 Professor John J. Tigert, reporting for the Committee on Student Welfare, told the faculty that the accomplishments of the honor system were very encouraging and urged that it be given their unqualified support.

At the close of the next school year, however, the plan was abandoned. Its failure had been due to two factors: unwillingness of students to report their fellows for cheating and other types of misconduct, and failure of the faculty to give it wholehearted support. Opponents among the teaching staff seem to have been quite sincere in their opposition. Among other things they disliked the requirement that teachers must leave the classrooms when tests were in progress. This was eventually made optional.

Proponents of the system, on the other hand, felt that this attitude indicated a lack of confidence in student government. They believed that without complete confidence the honor system could not possibly succeed.[4]

When Judge Barker came to the University in 1911, he encountered a traditional practice which caused him no little concern. Rivalry between freshman and sophomore classes usually reached a high pitch early in the fall and culminated in an annual flag rush. This attempt on the part of the men of each class to capture the other's flag usually developed into a free-for-all fight with some injuries on both sides. In the fall of 1911 Barker called the presidents of the two classes into conference and asked that they use their influence to bring this custom to an end. The combined effort was successful and no flag rush took place that year.

In the fall of the next year, with Barker out of town, the freshmen voted in favor of renewing the custom. Vice President White persuaded them to await the return of the President before taking any action. Upon his return Barker spoke to the assembled freshmen, giving his reasons for opposing a flag rush. Once again he was successful. The student newspaper commented thus: "The action of President Barker is always so manly and his ability as a mediator is so influential that the Freshmen decided to rescind their action of Monday and cease all further agitation of the subject. The opinion of President Barker," the writer continued, "is founded upon wisdom gained from long experience, and we urge the student body to stand behind him in this action."

4 Minutes of Faculty, October 23, 1911, June 1, 1912, June 7, 1913, March 5, 1915; Minutes of Board of Trustees, June 4, 1912; *Catalogue*, 1916-1917; Louisville *Courier-Journal*, February 3, December 8, 1911; Lexington *Herald*, June 13, 1916; Lexington *Leader*, January 27, 29, February 17, April 10, 27, September 14, 15, 1911, November 4, 1914; *The Kentucky Kernel*, January 11, April 26, 1917.

Although Judge Barker had opposed flag rushes, he realized that students needed an occasional outlet for their energies, and that class rivalry was an emotion not easy to kill. In 1913 he donated a heavy cable and suggested that freshmen and sophomores settle the question of relative strength by a tug of war. The cable was stretched across Clifton Pond a block east of the campus, and the members of the two classes seized opposite ends and began to pull. The freshmen got wet, and the sophomores celebrated victory by going downtown in a body.

In the following fall a half-day holiday was given, and the contest was held again. This time the freshmen by force of numbers dragged the sophomores through the pond. The same group of boys had lost two years in succession. Next morning the freshman flag was flying from the cupola of the gymnasium building, where it remained all day, an irritating reminder to the defeated second-year men. During the night the freshmen kept guards posted to prevent its removal, but the sophomores gathered their forces and easily routed the few guards and removed the flag.

By 1915 it was evident that lower division students did not consider the tug of war sufficient. The contest was scheduled for October 15, but before that day an unexpected melee between the two classes broke out. Late in September the freshmen under cover of darkness painted their class numerals on some of the buildings. Next day the sophomores procured several gallons of red paint and began painting over the numbers. Freshmen appeared and began to pelt the sophomores with small stones, bringing on what the student newspaper called "a general paint-smearing contest," which soon degenerated into a free-for-all.

The tug of war, when it came, brought the freshmen another victory. They celebrated by carrying the cable through the streets of downtown Lexington. This affair ended tragically, for as the group crossed Broadway at Third Street, a streetcar ran into the cable, knocking several students to the ground. One boy suffered a fractured skull and died a few hours later.

Hazing of freshmen was a problem on many campuses, and the University campus in Lexington was no exception. The Faculty from time to time passed resolutions condemning such practices, but enforcing them was difficult. The least harmful—but most prevalent—form of hazing was the cutting of hair. Town barbers willingly lent clippers, knowing that the damage done to the hair of freshmen by unskilled and none too gentle upperclassmen would bring most of the first-year men into their shops to have the remainder taken off. Cutting the hair of freshmen had long been considered a privilege of seniors. In September, 1915, Barker sent a letter to each senior reminding him that the Faculty had passed a rule against any form of hazing, and that the cutting of hair had been placed in this category. He mentioned also that in the preceding year many of them had signed a petition asking for the reinstatement of several students who had been suspended for hazing. The Faculty had honored this request on the basis of a promise made by the petitioners to refrain from and to discourage such activity in the future.

The seniors, being close to graduation, were inclined to cooperate, but the student newspaper carried an editorial expressing regret over the passing of a time-honored custom. "The wholesale destruction of Freshman foliage possessed many advantages," said the *Kernel*. "First, it lowered the beginner's estimate of his own importance and rendered his mind more receptive to the few bits of knowledge which he had overlooked while in high school, and must needs gather here. Second, it enabled the newcomers to 'get together,' thus inculcating a great amount of class spirit, and incidentally a large supply of college spirit. The University that possesses no class spirit will assuredly possess no college spirit." A few of the freshmen considered the cutting of their hair so important that they did the job themselves, but very soon the sophomores stepped into the breach left by the reformed and cooperative seniors.

When the President and members of the teaching staff came to work on the morning of September 25, they found on the sidewalks enough hair to cover the head of every man in the freshman class. A meeting of the discipline committee was set for the following Monday. Freshmen were urged to appear and if possible give the names of their tormentors. As a result of the investigation, four sophomores were expelled. A mass meeting of students was held and a strike was threatened. While this meeting was in progress, Judge Barker, according to the *Kernel*, "arrived with his fighting clothes on and fire in his eye. He told the students that if any of them wanted to be fired, just to let him know." This time the University authorities stood their ground.[5]

Possibly as a consequence of the war already raging in Europe, the University in the fall of 1915 began to enforce more strictly the requirement that all freshman and sophomore men participate in military drill. In his December report to the trustees President Barker said that the battalion consisted of "at least four hundred well-drilled young men, with a band of about thirty-five pieces." He expressed his opinion that in point of excellence it was

5 *The Kentucky Kernel*, September 16, 23, 30, 1915; Louisville *Courier-Journal*, September 26, 1915; Lexington *Leader*, September 29, 1911, October 12, 1914, October 16, 1915; *The Idea*, October 10, 1912, October 16, 1913; Minutes of Board of Trustees, December 14, 1915; Minutes of University Faculty, March 6, 20, 1914.

equal to that of any similar institution in the South or Southwest.

On October 25, 1916, Captain John C. Fairfax, Commandant of Cadets, brought to the attention of the Executive Committee of the Board of Trustees some provisions of the National Defense Act which had become law on June 3 of the same year. He recommended that the institution participate in the Reserve Officer Training Corps program which made it possible for a student to continue the study of Military Science and Tactics during his junior and senior years, and to receive a commission as a second lieutenant in the army reserve. After several meetings of the committee the proposal was accepted, March 21, 1917. The University of Kentucky was one of the first of the land grant colleges to take this step.[6]

Through their varied activities the students learned many things not made clear in books. They made friends, played with power, and fought equals roughly. They tried the patience of the faculty and the administration in their struggles between sport and study and in their defense of class and college spirit. The short life of their honor system showed how hard it was to bring in the new.

[6] Minutes of Board of Trustees, December 14, 1915; Minutes of Executive Committee, October 25, November 1, 1916, February 21, March 21, 1917; Lexington *Leader,* March 22, 1917.

CHAPTER III

SERVING THE COMMONWEALTH

A UNIVERSITY today is a complex institution. Perhaps it is now more accurately described by Clark Kerr's term, a "multiversity." Animating this complicated structure, however, is one function, that of service. Originally universities were expected to perform this function—sometimes thought of in a threefold way as the preserving, increasing, and transmitting of knowledge—within the limits of a campus, to their own students and faculty. The direct influence of a university has spread far beyond its campus, and with a state institution it is no exaggeration to say that its useful sphere is the whole state. This role of a university was slow in developing in Kentucky, and it was not until President Barker's administration that the University of Kentucky began to fulfill the implications of this role.

As might be expected from President Barker's belief that only by appealing to the farmers could the University secure financial support from the legislature, the College of Agriculture and the Agricultural Experiment Station had a leading part in extending the services of the University through the state. One endeavor was a cooperative plan of the University and the railroads for the benefit of farm families who might not be able to come to Lexington to attend any of the various programs offered for the improvement of agriculture and life on the farm. In March, 1911, the University, working with the Kentucky Department of Agriculture and the Southern Railroad, began sending agricultural demonstration trains to various parts of the state. The next year several railroads cooperated in sending a much longer train. The train made three or four stops each day, and crowds came aboard to inspect the exhibits, see the demonstrations, and hear the talks. Sometimes evening lectures were given in churches to larger groups of people. Several members of the agricultural faculty participated, as well as President Barker and the Kentucky Commissioner of Agriculture. In 1914 the Louisville and Nashville Railroad ran an exhibit train for the first time to eastern Kentucky.

During these years the Experiment Station was perhaps the most active area of the campus. Many of its staff members taught few, if any, classes, and the staff as a whole produced frequent bulletins and pamphlets. The Station undertook numerous experiments for improving tobacco, a leading cash crop, not only at Lexington, but also in other parts of the state. A plant for the production of hog cholera serum was erected, and the serum provided to Kentucky farmers at cost. Enough of this serum was sold outside the state to make the plant virtually self-sustaining. Other work at this time concerned the feeding of beef cattle, the diseases affecting poultry, infectious abortion in mares and cows, and infectious arthritis in colts. By 1914, the Experiment Station had leased seven plots of ground in other parts of the state and used these for experimental purposes and for demonstrating to farmers the advantages of using fertilizers, of crop rotation, and of improved methods of cultivation.

All work at the Experiment Station did not meet with approval, however. Some manufacturers of commercial fertilizers objected to bulletins critical of some of their products, saying these were causing the loss of sales. Professor Kastle insisted that the University had the right to publish the results of its investigations, and Barker supported him in this. He told the Board of Trustees that he regretted that the findings of the Experiment Station were contrary to the interests of some manufacturers but that he did not think any manufacturer should profit from the ignorance of the people and insist that information should be withheld from them.[1] While much of the work in agriculture produced tangible results, much of it produced results that could not so easily be reckoned, but it cannot be doubted that all these efforts served to make the University better known throughout the state. Notably some of this work—the demonstration trains, for instance—was done several years before the federal Smith-Lever Act became law.

Other colleges of the University were likewise expanding their services as well as making innovations in teaching techniques. The College of Mechanical and Electrical Engineering had an aggressive leader in Dean F. Paul Anderson, who made lengthy reports both to Barker and to the newspapers. In 1914 instead of requiring of each senior a written thesis, he introduced a plan that attracted considerable attention. The senior class was given the cooperative project of designing a power plant of sufficient size to furnish electricity for all of central and eastern Kentucky. Taking the town of Hazard as the theoretical location of the plant because of its convenience to water, transportation, and fuel, the students did all the work, from the initial surveys to the completion of drawings and specifications. The class of the following year designed a combined electric generating and central heating plant for the University.

[1] Minutes of Executive Committee, March 20, 1911, April 12, 1912, January 29, 1913, February 27, 1917; Minutes of Board of Trustees, December 12, 1911, December 12, 1912, December 9, 1913, December 8, 1914, June 9, December 14, 1915; Minutes of the Council, March 6, 1911; Reports of Joseph H. Kastle, May 16, 1913, May 18, 1915, Barker Papers; *The Idea,* January 10, 1913; Louisville *Courier-Journal,* November 28, 1911, December 20, 1912; Lexington *Leader,* December 17, 1911, January 10, June 9, 1913, January 11, 1915, February 16, 1916.

The Dean of the College of Civil Engineering, Walter E. Rowe, sometimes rivaled Anderson in seeking public support. He stressed the importance of transportation, saying that a thing had to be in a certain place at a certain time in order for it to possess value. Besides its normal work in training professional engineers, the College of Civil Engineering introduced a special ten-week course in road building in 1911. Each county judge in the state could appoint two men to take this course, the only expense being for room and board. Not all counties took advantage of this opportunity, to be sure; but by the 1915 session 153 men were in attendance. Outside speakers included public officials and representatives of corporations that engaged in highway construction. By 1917 a short program for city engineers had been added. Smaller cities in particular were urged to send representatives. Engineers from the larger cities were asked to serve as instructors.

In an address to the General Assembly in 1912 Governor James B. McCreary spoke well of the contributions being made to the state by the colleges of engineering at the University. He cited particularly the work of the College of Civil Engineering and that of Mining Engineering.

Under the guidance of Dean Charles J. Norwood the curriculum of the College of Mining Engineering had been designed to meet the needs of as many Kentuckians as possible. The University offered four-year courses leading to the degrees of Mining Engineer and Metallurgical Engineer, a two-year course, and an annual eight-week course for practical miners. In addition, extension classes were organized among the men and boys in the coal mining towns of southeastern Kentucky. Dean Norwood was especially proud of the eight-week course in which the instructors tried to provide individual instruction that allowed for differences in background and ability. Many of the men who took this course became mine foremen, leaders among their associates. In endeavors such as the eight-week course, Dean Norwood thought that he and his faculty not only were providing technical education but also were offering social betterment to the miners.[2]

On the campus at Lexington the early years of the Barker administration saw other changes in the University. In 1913 the College of Law introduced evening classes for the benefit of those who had to work during the day but wished to gain a degree in law. Several prominent Lexington attorneys, among them Richard C. Stoll, Samuel Wilson, Charles Kerr, William H. Townsend, and William E. Nichols, gave lectures to the law students during these years. Also begun about this time was a course of instruction for prospective athletic coaches, given by Edwin R. Sweetland, the Director of Athletics. Reflecting the times was a class, planned by Dean Anderson, in the manufacture, care, and driving of automobiles, and unusual for this time was the course in English for foreigners which was offered under the guidance of Dean Mackenzie. The Barker administration also saw the revival of summer school at the University. Summer work, largely for the benefit of public school teachers, soon became a permanent part of the University's program. Beginning in 1913, Professor J. T. C. Noe, perhaps better known as Cotton, served as director. The sessions of 1914 and 1916 were attended by over 150 students each.

The University Library in this six-year period gave

[2] Louisville *Courier-Journal*, March 7, 8, 9, 1911, January 3, 1912, Lexington *Leader*, March 17, 1912, October 20, 1913, February 18, July 5, 16, 1914, September 12, 1915; Anderson's Report to Barker, August 15, 1915, Rowe's Report to Barker, June, 1915, and Norwood's Report to Barker, June 4, 1915, all in Barker Papers; Minutes of Executive Committee, January 17, 1917.

impressive signs of growth in that the total number of books increased 70 percent. But appearances can be misleading. At the end of this period the total number of volumes was only 33,869. Of greater importance was the fact that in the summer of 1912 the books were catalogued, and at the beginning of the fall term of this year students for the first time were allowed to check them out.

Although the University expanded its areas of service under President Barker, research and publication by the faculty were limited. For the most part this was due to the heavy teaching loads, but it was also due, in some instances, to lack of desire and even to lack of training. Two of the most productive scholars at the University during these years were Dean Mackenzie, whose *Evolution of Literature* was published in 1911, and Professor Kastle, who at the time of his death had published about one hundred articles in chemistry journals and had been co-author of one book. Other scholars of this period whose work had gained them recognition were Professor Lyman Chalkley of the College of Law, who published a three-volume work, *Chronicles of the Scotch-Irish Settlement in Virginia,* and Dr. Joseph W. Pryor, who had done extensive research on the ossification of bones.

The growth of the University during the early Barker administration is reflected not only in its increased services to the people of Kentucky, but also in the greatly increased enrollments. The regular session grew from a total of 582 in the academic year 1910-1911 to a total of 998 in 1916-1917, a growth of which President Barker was justifiably proud. In a report to the Board of Trustees, he commented favorably on the quality of these students, attributing it to the work of the University with the high school teachers over the state. He went on to point out to the trustees the favorable position University students had gained in oratorical and debating contests and in national agricultural shows. The College of Mechanical and Electrical Engineering and the College of Law were likewise highly regarded parts of the University.[3]

The growing enrollment of which Barker was so proud and the expanding services of the University, however, meant increased costs, and also increased indebtedness, if the state did not awaken to the University's needs. Barker's administration had inherited a debt of about $50,000, to which was added in 1910-1911 some $13,000 and in 1911-1912 about $21,000. Therefore Barker's years at the University were marked by the struggle to secure financial support, to persuade the people of Kentucky that higher education was a public responsibility.

In seeking support, Judge Barker went outside the state and opened negotiations with both the General Education Board and the Peabody Education Fund. Although Dr. Wallace Buttrick of the General Education Board came to Lexington and visited the University, this Rockefeller-endowed foundation made no grant. Dr. Wickliffe Rose looked over the University for the Peabody Fund. This foundation gave $40,000 toward the support of the University's School of Education with the understanding that the income from this endowment, likely to amount to about $2,000 a year, would be supplemented by a sufficient sum to make a total of $10,000 annually. These terms the University Board of Trustees gladly accepted.

In his appeals to the legislature, Barker made much of the contributions of the University to agriculture in the state. In 1912 he and Dean Scovell used this as the basis of their request for funds and received for the next bien-

[3] *The Idea,* April 6, May 11, 1911, September 12, 19, 1912, December 18, 1913; *The Kentucky Kernel,* May 11, 18, 1916; Lexington *Leader,* March 15, June 11, November 3, 1911, January 31, February 2, March 8, 1912, August 23, 1914, July 2, December 3, 17, 1916; Louisville *Courier-Journal,* January 3, 1912; *Catalogue,* 1912-1913; *The University of Kentucky: Its History and Development* (Lexington, 1956), pp. 22, 26, 30.

nium an appropriation of a little over $490,000. Later that year Barker remarked that the agricultural departments should be developed as fast and as far as possible, thereby strengthening the appeal to the farmers, who were the dominant group in the General Assembly. Two years later Barker slanted his argument in a different direction. It was commonly thought, he said, that the legislature had spent great sums of money upon the University. The State Auditor's report from 1880 to 1913 showed that the state had given the University the total of $2,199,224, which averaged out to a little less than $67,000 for each of the thirty-three years, hardly generous support even for the times. Moreover, states like Illinois, Wisconsin, and Minnesota were giving their universities more in a single year than Kentucky had given for all thirty-three years. Moving closer to home, Barker pointed out that in the fiscal year 1912-1913 the city of Louisville had spent almost $50,000 more on its Male High School than the entire state had spent on the University. Barker's argument evidently failed to stir the complacency of the legislators, for the appropriation for the coming biennium was somewhat smaller than for the previous one—a little under $473,000. In commenting to the trustees on this disappointing appropriation, President Barker reiterated his opinion that the University must make itself useful to the state before it could receive the financial support necessary to make it a great university.[4]

While to the legislature Barker emphasized the usefulness of the University to the state and particularly to the farmers, to the Board of Trustees and, of course, through it, indirectly, to the state administration, he made a point

4 Wickliffe Rose to Barker, November 13, 1911, Barker to Rose, November 23, 1911, Barker Papers; Minutes of Executive Committee, October 23, 1911, March 25, 1914; Minutes of Board of Trustees, December 12, 1911, June 4, December 12, 1912, June 4, December 8, 1914, June 9, 1915.

of the economy with which the University was operated. Reporting to the board in 1915, he said that the average cost per student at twenty-two other state universities—for which he submitted figures—was $310 while at Kentucky it was only $150. Furthermore, an inquiry sent to various universities showed that most of them required no more than fifteen hours a week of classroom teaching; some of these schools even stated that they would not accept the work of an institution which exceeded this teaching load. But the faculty at Kentucky, Barker told the trustees, averaged eighteen hours a week in the classroom, and, from all aspects, the University was accomplishing more work at less cost than any similar institution he knew of. But he did not go into the question of the quality of the work which was being done.

The University's agricultural program was greatly strengthened by the passage of the federal Smith-Lever Act of 1914. Under the terms of this measure, $480,000 was appropriated for each year, this to be divided equally among the states. An additional $600,000 was to be made available in the second year, and $500,000 for each of the next seven years, thus bringing the total annual appropriation to $4,100,000 in addition to the original $480,000 for each year. The latter was to be divided equally, but in the case of the former there were two additional provisions. First, it was to be divided in accordance with the ratio which the rural population of a given state bore to the total rural population. In the second place the amount due a state had to be matched by an equal contribution from the state or from some agency or individual within the state.

Fortunately the Agricultural Extension Department had sufficient funds to match the federal offer until July 1, 1916. After that time it would be up to the legislature to make the necessary appropriations. Barker told the trustees that he was confident that upon a proper presentation of the needs of the farmers, the legislature would provide enough funds to enable the state to enjoy the whole amount which should come to it under the Smith-Lever Act. In this assumption his confidence was not misplaced. At its 1916 session the Kentucky General Assembly accepted the terms of the federal legislation. The regular state appropriation for the 1916-1918 biennium was increased slightly, for the first time exceeding $500,000.

The Smith-Hughes Act of 1917 continued the dollar matching principle. By encouraging the teaching of vocational subjects, including agriculture and home economics, in the high schools, the act made necessary the training of teachers in these fields and provided money for this purpose. As a result the University instituted Departments of Vocational Education, Agricultural Education, and Home Economics Education.

The physical plant and equipment underwent only a moderate increase during the Barker administration. In 1911 the University acquired a house adjoining the Patterson Hall grounds and converted part of it into a badly needed student infirmary. In the same year the Executive Committee authorized the construction of a system of sewers for the University. The only major building of the Barker period was an addition to the Experiment Station. This was dedicated on June 3, 1913, and a portrait of the late Dr. Scovell was presented to the University, followed a year later by a plaque done by Lorado Taft and featuring a life-size bust of Scovell.

The greatly increased enrollments during Barker's presidency resulted in a natural increase in costs. But, added to this, his otherwise commendable policy of extending the University's services throughout the state created a financial dilemma for his administration, for these services, apparently motivated to a large extent by Barker's desire to appeal to the legislature for more funds, increased further the University's operating costs. The legislature, however, was not sufficiently moved to raise its appropriations to an adequate level as compared with a number of other states; and though the chief executives of the state urged greater support upon the legislature, none of them during this time pushed this actively. More importantly, no attempt seems to have been made to find an added source of revenue that might be used for the University. Whether Barker's somewhat narrow conception of the uses of a university in society as a whole played a significant part in the matter of support or whether both he and those to whom he appealed for support were simply in their views representative of the temper of the times—these are perhaps open questions. His claim of virtue for economy, particularly as it was reflected in heavy teaching loads, is more open to criticism. But whatever faults Barker may have had as President, it cannot be denied that during his administration the University began to reach more widely into the Commonwealth both in its training of greater numbers of students on the Lexington campus and in the efforts of the agricultural and engineering schools over the whole state.

The Smith-Lever Act aided somewhat the financial situation of the University, and the legislature did provide somewhat increased funds. Differences between the earnings of various faculty members, however, coupled with the growing prestige of certain departments, were creating a spirit of professional jealousy on the campus, and the final days of Barker as President were marked by strife which hurt the faculty, the administration, and, ultimately, the students.

CHAPTER IV

SIXTY-NINE RECOMMENDATIONS

FROM his disagreement with President Emeritus Patterson and from the protests raised over the attempted merger of two of the engineering colleges early in his tenure, no great discernment was needed to see that President Barker's administrative abilities were likely to be severely tested in the years to come. Problems were perhaps natural in a growing institution, and if Barker had had a better background in administration, they would probably not have reached the magnitude which they did. As it was, however, the disputes which arose dissipated energies that might have gone to better use, and in the end they brought about Barker's resignation from the University.

One such disagreement occurred in the College of Agriculture, where the Smith-Lever Act made provision for a gradual expansion of the University's agricultural extension work, but Dean Kastle and the Superintendent of the Department of Agricultural Extension, Fred Mutchler, could not agree on how this work was to be carried out. The two men were invited to appear before the Executive Committee and present their views. No immediate settlement was reached. At its meeting on October 15, 1915, the Executive Committee directed that Kastle, Barker, and a board member go to Washington to discuss the matter with the State Relations Committee of the Department of Agriculture. In Washington these three men from Kentucky reached an agreement with the Department of Agriculture regarding each of the current extension projects in Kentucky.

At this point Kastle's health failed, and he asked to be

relieved of the deanship but to continue as Director of the Experiment Station. Professor George Roberts was appointed as acting dean, and in less than a month, Kastle was dead. Alfred M. Peter now became acting Director of the Experiment Station. This left Mutchler in a stronger position than before. His title was changed to Director of Agricultural Extension. Early in January, 1917, Roberts complained to Barker and the Executive Committee that Mutchler did not confer with him on any matter relating to the extension services. The attitude of acting Director Alfred M. Peter of the Experiment Station was quite different. He readily admitted that his was a division of the College of Agriculture and acted accordingly.

At its meeting on January 17, 1916, the Executive Committee received a petition from twenty-six members of the College of Agriculture, the Experiment Station, and Agricultural Extension Department, stressing the need for close cooperation among the three areas, approved it, and ordered it spread upon the minutes. No dean was selected, but Barker informed both Peter and Mutchler that the committee's action meant that Roberts as acting dean was to have general supervision over their work. Peter continued to cooperate, but Mutchler continued to act as if he were the head of a division not subject to Roberts' authority.[1]

At the beginning of Barker's administration, the Board

---

[1] Minutes of Executive Committee, August 25, October 15, 1915, August 29, November 15, 1916, January 17, 1917; *Catalogue*, 1916-1917, pp. 16-19; Kastle to Barker, September 25, 1915, Mary E. Sweeney to Kastle, February 28, 1915, Kastle to Barker, May 18, 1915, Barker to Kastle, May 19, 1915, Kastle to Mutchler, June 24, 1915, Kastle to Barker, June 24, 1915, Mutchler to Bradford Knapp, October 16, 1915, Kastle to Barker and Executive Committee, November 15, 1915, George Roberts to Barker and Executive Committee, January 12, 1917, Staff of College of Agriculture to Barker and Board of Trustees, January 10, 1917, Barker to Peter and Mutchler, January 24, 1917, Roberts to Mutchler, March 15, 1917, Mutchler to Roberts, April 23, 1917, Barker Papers.

of Trustees consisted of eighteen members. During his years in office there were changes in the constitution of this body. From time to time alumni had proposed that they be represented on the board, and on March 20, 1914, the Governor signed a bill increasing the board by six members, these six new members to be elected by graduates of the University. In addition, three of the other fifteen appointive members were to be alumni. On the Executive Committee, which the bill increased from five to seven members, three members should be alumni. This measure gave the alumni its voice in the affairs of the University surely, but at the price of a more unwieldly Board of Trustees. Later, in 1916, the legislature increased the size of the board even further by adding eight more ex officio members—the Commissioner of Agriculture, Labor, and Statistics and the seven members of the State Board of Agriculture.[2]

The crucial move in President Barker's administration, however, was his recommendation to the Executive Committee in 1916 and the committee's subsequent vote that the Colleges of Civil Engineering and of Mechanical and Electrical Engineering be merged under Dean Anderson. This provoked a bitter report from Dean Rowe of Civil Engineering, which appeared in the Lexington *Herald*, and three weeks later the appearance of circulars on the campus criticizing Barker's election as President of the University.

When the Board of Trustees met on December 12, 1916, Barker discussed the proposed merger, in which the College of Mines and Metallurgy had asked to be included. Barker pointed out that consolidation would

[2] Barker to Harold Amos, February 1, 1913, McCreary to Barker, October 8, 1913, Barker to McCreary, October 10, 1913, Barker Papers; Kentucky General Assembly, *Acts*, 1914, p. 174, *Acts*, 1916, p. 149; Lexington *Leader*, March 20, 1914, July 2, 1916; *The Kentucky Kernel*, September 21, 1916; Minutes of Executive Committee, July 19, 1916.

enable the University to use the total available space to the best advantage and save the cost of providing a new building.   In conclusion he said that one of the great handicaps of the University was the spirit of rivalry existing among the three engineering colleges. "This sort of spirit does harm to all students and should be eliminated." Dean Rowe and a number of students with petitions were then admitted to the meeting.   At the end of his remarks Dean Rowe suggested that the board appoint a committee to investigate fully the situation before it took any action.[3]

In January, 1917, the Governor appointed an Investigating Committee of five members of the board—not on the Executive Committee and not residents of Lexington or Fayette County.   As this committee realized that it would need professional aid, it engaged a three-member Survey Commission, consisting of men of experience in higher education.   Two of them were former university presidents, and the third was the registrar of the University of Illinois.   The job done by the Investigating Committee was thorough.   It interviewed 150 witnesses— students, faculty, alumni, citizens of Lexington, and other citizens from widely divergent parts of the state.   In addition to answering questions, witnesses were given a chance to present other information.   Questionnaires were sent to 1,600 alumni asking, among other things, for opinions on discipline at the University, the "moral influence of the faculty," the advisability of combining the engineering colleges, and the qualifications which the President of the University should have to assure a successful administration.   About 350 replies were received from the alumni. Six hundred questionnaires were sent to representative

3 Minutes of the Executive Committee, November 15, 1916; Minutes of Board of Trustees, December 12, 1916; Lexington *Herald*, November 16, 1916; Lexington *Leader*, December 7, 1916; Pritchett to Barker, January 26, 1910, Stoll to Barker, November 16, 1916, copy of extract from Sixth Annual Report of Carnegie Foundation, Barker Papers.

citizens, asking what kind of reputation the University had in their communities and what additional services the University might well render. They also asked these citizens why parents sent their children to schools other than the University of Kentucky, and received about a hundred answers. The oral testimony taken by the committee filled 1,128 typewritten pages.

The Survey Commission of three rendered invaluable assistance, meeting with the Investigating Committee from time to time, inspecting buildings, laboratories, dormitories, and the library, and examining records of the business agent and the registrar. This commission also conferred with thirty-four staff members, including Patterson, Barker, and all the deans, with seven seniors, and with several members of the Board of Trustees. It also made a long report to the Investigating Committee, and this was incorporated in the committee's report to the board.

The commission's first recommendation was for a reduction in the size of the board from thirty-two to fifteen members, so that it might be less difficult to obtain a quorum. It also recommended that the board should keep in closer touch with the University by holding quarterly meetings, publishing its minutes and those of the Executive Committee, sending them to all administrative officers and heads of departments, and to any citizen of Kentucky on request. This might help to allay the feeling of suspicion among faculty and citizens that things were wrong in high places of the institution.

The commission reported that the lack of an adequate conception of the presidency had been the one most important cause of the difficulties in which the University had become entangled. The relationship between the President and the Board of Trustees should be clearly defined and stated in the by-laws. The President should be an educational expert in the fullest sense of the term, thoroughly experienced in University administration, able to diagnose difficulties readily and to see the source of those difficulties, to recommend to the board proper measures for meeting emergencies, and able to carry out the board's wishes with energy and skill. The commission reached the conclusion that President Barker was not such an educational expert and had never professed to be one. "We are convinced," said the report, "that the welfare of the University and of the State which it serves demand his retirement at an early date to make way for a professional educational administrator."

The report spoke of Judge Barker as having been in an impossible situation, that of the captain of a ship without having ever studied navigation. Yet he had brought to his duties "a largeness of soul . . . a loyalty to his friends and a charity for his enemies which are beyond praise." The members of the commission were convinced that his chances to succeed would have been improved if in the past six years he had not had to contend with the insistent presence of James K. Patterson. For the sake of the next President, they recommended that the President Emeritus be requested to resign from the Board of Trustees and evacuate the President's House.

As to internal organization, the investigation showed that the Council, through certain gradual changes, had become a committee of academic deans and had usurped some powers of the Faculty. The commission recommended that the Council as originally constituted be revived and that the registrar be included in its membership as secretary ex officio.

The report of the Survey Commission was not limited to criticism and suggested changes. It praised especially the office of the registrar, Ezra L Gillis, where the commission found a set of records and a system of administration which, considering the possibilities, "are not in our judgment surpassed at any other state university." It was recommended that the registrar be given full charge of admissions and class scheduling, with the understanding that he would be acting as the administrative agent of the Faculty.[4]

The commission gave some attention to the problem of members of the faculty accepting employment outside the University. It suggested that a distinction be made between work which would help to keep the faculty member up to date in his field and work which did not increase his proficiency, but did cause him to neglect his obligation to the University. Dean Anderson's outside work was so well known that the commission was not hesitant about using it as an example. Some of his outside work was considered legitimate, and some was not. His service as consulting engineer for the Queen and Crescent Railway was considered desirable, as it was the type of expert service that members of the staff should sometimes render. On the other hand, his partnership work as an architect, with offices in Mechanical Hall, doing all the firm's work there and working in direct competition with other Lexington architects, was strongly criticized by the commission.

The commission also had some words to say on the county-appointee law. Their conclusion was that this law was not accomplishing its purpose and should be repealed. Political considerations entered into some of the appointments. Students often failed to receive the appointments which they expected, and many of them grew angry and went to some other institution or did not go to college at all. The conclusion was reached that the law kept away more students than it attracted. Furthermore it neces-

4 "Report of the Investigating Committee," *Bulletin of the University of Kentucky,* IX (July, 1917), 1-8, 10-24.

sitated that the University maintain dormitories for men as well as for women. The existing men's dormitories the commission regarded as a disgrace.

As for the problem that had led directly to the appointment of the Investigating Committee and the Survey Commission—the unsolved issue of whether or not to consolidate the three engineering colleges—the commission recommended that the three be consolidated under one dean, hired from outside the University, with the deans of the three colleges remaining but working as department heads.

In agriculture there was a slightly different problem because the difficulty did not concern three coordinate colleges, but the College of Agriculture and its two affiliates, the Agricultural Extension Service and the Agricultural Experiment Station, each of the two latter under a director who was responsible to the Dean of the College of Agriculture. While the commission was at work trying to adjust related organizations, the members of the agricultural staffs had worked out their own pattern of organization and had secured approval in January, 1917. Both of the directors were to be responsible to the Dean of the College of Agriculture. Seeing that one of the directors found it hard to take directions from the dean, the commission recommended that the Dean of the College of Agriculture and the two directors responsible to him be notified of the reaffirmation of their agreement, and that the directors receive a statement that if either director made an appointment or any expenditure of funds not already authorized, or took any action involving a change of policy without approval of the dean, it would be regarded as an act of insubordination and a proper cause for dismissal.

The Survey Commission had words of praise for the School of Education but recommended that it be expanded. The professor of secondary education, McHenry Rhoads, was doing excellent work in his additional duty as high school supervisor. Much credit was given to him for increase in the number of accredited high schools from 83 in 1910 to 221 in 1917. It seemed, however, that he should be given one or more assistants. "The proposition that 120 counties, 40,181 square miles, is too much for one man to cover . . . needs only to be stated to be accepted. It is not unlike putting a single man into the field to do the agricultural extension work for the entire state." In the Department of Education a Model High School had been authorized, but had not actually been established. The Commission's report suggested that a school of education without its practice school was like a department of chemistry without a laboratory. It recommended that as soon as possible a practice high school for the School of Education—wholly under the control of the University—be established.

Both the Investigating Committee and the Survey Commission heard much criticism of the discipline at the University, but it was hard to blame any individual or group. President Barker had tried to make student government work before a sufficient number of students were ready for this new freedom. Several faculty members testified that Barker was "too big-hearted" and that students took advantage of this fact.[5]

The Survey Commission's report on the degrees held by University of Kentucky faculty members in 1917 gives at least a partial picture of the quality of the institution. The faculty had a total of 176 degrees conferred by 61 institutions. Sixty-seven of these degrees had been conferred by the University of Kentucky. Among the degrees

[5] "Report of the Investigating Committee," pp. 31-44, 53-56, 93-95; Lynn B. Evans to Henry S. Barker, April 2, 1917, Barker Papers; "Testimony Taken by Special Investigating Committee," I, 20-25, 44, 47-49, 56-57, 322-23, 330, II, 25-36, 112-33, 242, 247, 637-38.

of the faculty were ten Ph.D.'s, six being in the Chemistry School, four M.D.'s, twenty-eight M.A.'s, twenty-four M.S.'s, six M.E.'s, three C.E.'s, and one E.E. Very few of the faculty belonged to honor societies, two being members of Phi Beta Kappa, seven of Sigma Xi, and three of Tau Beta Pi. Five were listed in *Who's Who in America* and seven in *American Men of Science.*

A second indication of quality, or the lack of it, is found in the limited amount of faculty publication. Seven books had been published by five men, and four more were said to be in preparation. Twenty-two men had published a total of eighty-three articles in standard journals. One hundred eighty-five articles had appeared as bulletins or in minor publications. The comment of the commission was that all things considered, the results might have been expected to be considerably greater.

This rather thorough survey revealed a few examples of nepotism, but not as many as were expected. Far more serious was the matter of inbreeding. Not only had 67 of the 176 faculty degrees been conferred by the University of Kentucky, but also the greater part of the faculty's teaching experience had been obtained at this one institution. The College of Mechanical and Electrical Engineering provided an extreme example. Its teaching staff had a total of 129 years of experience, of which 126 years had been obtained at this University. All of them had obtained their degrees at Kentucky. The commission referred to this as "an example of so-called 'inbreeding' which would have few parallels."

The Investigating Committee accepted the recommendations of the Survey Commission with three exceptions. The committee would delay the combining of the engineering colleges until a new President had been in active charge for one year. This was to give him an opportunity to study the case of Dean Anderson so that Anderson would not be eliminated from consideration for the deanship of the new and larger college.

After sifting all the evidence regarding Dean Rowe, the committee decided to recommend his retirement. This was based not only upon his having given misleading information about his scholastic attainments, but also upon his failure to take any action in regard to letters which had been copied and distributed around the campus, apparently by civil engineering students.

In the case of President Emeritus Patterson the committee agreed that he should be asked to move his residence from the campus but felt that he might be allowed to remain on the Board of Trustees so long as his presence there did not hamper the new administration.

Based on its own study and the suggestions of the Survey Commission, the Investigating Committee made to the board in its June meeting, 1917, a report consisting of sixty-nine recommendations. The first of these was that President Barker's retirement should take effect September 1, 1918, and the second advocated Patterson's immediate removal from the campus. The chairman of the board was asked to appoint a committee consisting of four board members and three faculty members to nominate a new President. Other recommendations had to do with the making of appointments strictly on the basis of merit, without being influenced by political, religious, fraternal, or family connections. In an effort to reduce the amount of inbreeding, a provision was made against the employment of an alumnus for more than two years unless he had been employed elsewhere for as much as five years. The board accepted all but one of the recommendations of its Investigating Committee. The suggestion that Patterson be required to remove his residence from the campus was defeated by a vote of 11 to 5 with several members not voting.

The investigation, a serious matter, was conducted in a dignified way. Nevertheless, the Class of 1917 in its annual, *The Kentuckian*, could not resist a little humor. In a parody of the efforts of the governor's committee to get at the bottom of charges of misconduct of the University's affairs, the witty article asked whether the reader thought that economy and efficiency would be promoted by painting the messhall green instead of white, or that a more efficient distribution of the University's cuspidors could be made, or that the dormitories would make good cattle barns if properly ventilated. The jesting continued by passing a sentence upon those who could not answer these questions, *viz.*, that they be required to take a semester of mathematics under Professor J. Morton Davis, who, though kindly, was noted for being rigorous.[6]

The board and its Executive Committee promptly started work on the recommendations which they had accepted, and Judge Barker gave them his loyal support. Dr. Paul Boyd, who had just been named as Dean of the College of Arts and Science, was asked to serve as acting President whenever Barker should be absent, in case he did not remain on the campus until the arrival of his successor. Arthur M. Miller, Boyd's predecessor, had requested a leave of absence and had stated that when he returned he preferred to limit his activity to the teaching of geology.

During the 1917 investigation a favorite subject had been the indispensable qualifications of a university president. As to his education he must have both undergraduate and graduate training, thorough experience in

6 "Testimony Taken by Special Investigating Committee," II, 23-25; "Report of Investigating Committee," pp. 58-62, 93-97, 103-11; Minutes of Board of Trustees, June 7, 1917; Minutes of Executive Committee, June 20, 1917; *The Kentuckian*, 1917, p. 311; Minutes of Faculty, June 11, 1917; Lexington *Leader*, June 12, 1917; William A. Ganfield to Barker, July 23, 1917, Barker Papers.

university administration, ability to speak with authority on higher educational principles, to diagnose the difficulties and carry out the will of the board with energy and skill. Yet in personality he must have a largeness of soul, a tolerance of enemies, and freedom from professional jealousy. Now the question was who would fill the place which Barker's resignation would leave vacant?

CHAPTER V

A NEW PRESIDENT

WHEN the Board of Trustees of the University of Kentucky met on August 15, 1917, the nominating committee was ready to make its report. The members had conferred with leading educators in many parts of the country and with the representatives of educational foundations, and they had interviewed numerous suggested candidates. They now recommended that the position be offered to Dr. Frank L. McVey, President of the University of North Dakota.

A native of Ohio, Dr. McVey had graduated at Ohio Wesleyan University in 1893. He received his Ph.D. in economics at Yale in 1895, and after a year as an instructor at Columbia, he moved to the University of Minnesota, where he was made an assistant professor of economics in 1898 and a full professor in 1900. In 1907 he left the university to become chairman of the Minnesota Tax Commission, and in 1909 he became President of the University of North Dakota. In this year he served as vice president of the American Economic Association. He had already found time to publish three books and twenty articles and to study in England. In 1912 he delivered a series of lectures at the University of Christiana and spent the remainder of that summer touring Europe and studying German cooperatives.

Of all the presidential possibilities considered by the committee, McVey was one of the few who had not been a candidate for the position. His selection had been based in a large measure upon his record as President of the University of North Dakota. The historian of that institution gave an admirable one-sentence appraisal when he said: "In the years to come the faculty that he had left, recalling with nostalgia the great days of McVey, would establish them as the standard of measurement for future administrations." The nominating committee recommended that the new President receive a salary of $8,750 and that a residence on the Mulligan property, east of the University, be made into a President's home, and Dr. McVey accepted the presidency, officially taking office on September 1, 1917.[1]

Dr. McVey came to the University of Kentucky with a full understanding of the immensity of the task which lay ahead. The thorough work of the Investigating Committee and the Survey Commission provided a detailed analysis of the problems to be solved. In congratulating him, a member of the commission wrote: "It's a man's sized job, McVey, and will need all your inches, patience, tact, and vision."

McVey made several trips to Lexington before he was able to make it his permanent residence. His research and writing required that much of his time this autumn be spent in Washington, and he had accepted the position with that understanding. His first visit was for a week in September, when he went over the budget, visited many of the buildings, and had private conferences with some of the department heads. On this visit he made his first address to the student body of the University.

In mid-October he spent another week in Lexington, attended his first faculty meeting in the University, and spoke again to the students. Here at the student convocation he continued the practice which he had followed at

[1] Louis G. Geiger, *University of the Northern Plains* (Grand Forks, N. D., 1958), 192-93, 215, 234-35; E. J. James to McVey, August 18, 1917, Enoch Grehan to McVey, August 16, 1917, and McVey to Grehan, August 20, 1917, McVey Papers; Ezra Gillis notes in University of Kentucky Archives; Minutes of Board of Trustees, August 15, 1917.

the University of North Dakota of holding a "Between-us Day" and indicated that he would call two such meetings each semester. This was his way of keeping students informed on important matters and of securing their support in his effort to make the University what it ought to be. Returning to Lexington in November for a few days, he announced that he would soon be through with his monograph. He also took time to address the Kentucky Press Association and a state conference of the YMCA. At a meeting of the trustees in December he was able to report that he had met four times with the Executive Committee, four times with the faculty, and three with the University Council. He had also met with representatives of the two Normal Schools in regard to the courses to be offered under the Smith-Hughes Act. All this was in addition to numerous committee meetings at the University. Although he had been officially the President of the University since September 1, 1917, his formal inauguration did not take place until June 4, 1918, when the close of the academic year was at hand.

After American entry into the first World War, the University like many others had to make arrangements for students entering the armed services, and it took part in training others for the war effort. On April 9, 1917, the Executive Committee of the Board of Trustees voted to give to any senior who entered the armed forces his degree at the June commencement without further examination. Those enlistees from the other classes upon return from service might enter the next higher class. The faculty passed a resolution giving full credit for the semester to students who returned to farm homes to help in producing food for the war effort. Some engineering students left school to work in defense plants, while a limited number were allowed to enter the enlisted reserve corps. This

FRANK LeROND McVEY

placed them in class five in the draft and enabled them to continue and in some cases to finish their college program. By the end of April half of the men who had been in residence had left the campus. The grounds of the Kentucky Trotting Horse Breeders' Association were turned over to the University and became an army camp. Beginning in the fall term, 1918, all able-bodied students of the University were in one of four organizations: the ROTC, the Naval Training Unit, the Enlisted Reserve Corps, or the Students' Army Training Corps. Superior students were allowed to complete their course; those whose work was poor might be transferred to active duty. By this time the enlistment of professors was being discouraged on the ground that they were doing essential and highly specialized work.

The signing of the armistice brought a surprisingly swift and smooth transition from a wartime to a peacetime university program. Many of the men who had come as soldiers or sailors remained as civilian students. During the period of American participation in the war the University of Kentucky had trained 1,925 men, 1,289 in vocational work and 636 in regular college work.[2]

One of McVey's first problems as President was finding a dean for the College of Agriculture, which had lacked firm leadership since the death of Dean Scovell. After some search, McVey nominated Thomas P. Cooper, Director of the Experiment Station of the North Dakota Agricul-

2 Minutes of Board of Trustees, June 4, September 18, December 10, 1918, June 17, 1919; Lexington *Leader*, September 15, 30, October 5, 18, November 20, 22, 1917, January 2, 4, February 12, June 19, August 14, September 3, 4, 1918; Lexington *Herald*, September 16, October 10, 1917, January 29, July 15, 1918; *The Kentucky Kernel*, September 14, 1917, May 9, 1918; McVey Diary, December 14, 1939, March 14, 1941, June 29, 1942; Geiger, *University of the Northern Plains*, 262; Kendric C. Babcock to McVey, September 5, 1917, McVey Papers; Minutes of Executive Committee, September 19, November 21, 1917, June 10, 1918.

tural College at Fargo. Cooper's nomination was promptly approved by the full Board of Trustees, and he arrived in Lexington immediately to take up his new duties in January, 1918. Cooper proved to be an excellent choice for the position, and in the following year, after the resignation of Fred Mutchler, he was given the additional title of Director of Agricultural Extension.

In fact, McVey moved to strengthen the entire faculty as rapidly as possible. In 1918 there were several additions, including among them William D. Funkhouser, a Cornell Ph.D. who became the head of the Department of Zoology, Edward Wiest, a Columbia Ph.D. who was brought in to head the Department of Economics and Sociology, Charles S. Crouse, professor of metallurgy, Ernest A. Bureau, assistant professor of electrical engineering, and Carl A. Lampert, head of the Department of Music. A year later Harry Best, Ph.D., became professor of sociology; William W. Dimock, D.V.M., became head of the Department of Veterinary Science; William D. Valleau, Ph.D., was hired as assistant professor of plant pathology; and Morris Scherago, D.V.M., was appointed instructor in bacteriology.

Among the 1920 additions were Flora E. LeStourgeon, Ph.D., assistant professor of mathematics, Charles Barkenbus, Ph.D., assistant professor of chemistry, and J. Catron Jones, assistant professor of history and political science, who eventually became head of a separate Department of Political Science. In 1921 Frank T. McFarland, a member of the Botany Department who had just obtained his Ph.D., became department head. James B. Miner, Ph.D., became head of the Department of Psychology in the same year, and Grant C. Knight was hired as instructor in English. The year 1922 saw the addition of William L. Roberts, J.D., as professor of law, William R. Allen, Ph.D., as assistant professor of zoology, and Arthur C. McFarlan,

Ph.D., as assistant professor of geology. When Judge
Barker became President of the University of Kentucky,
only six faculty members held Ph.D. degrees; by 1922
twenty-two of them held this degree.[3]

The new President was quick to bring to the attention
of the Board of Trustees the need for higher salaries.
Postwar prices had lowered the purchasing power of the
dollar at a time when the University would need to increase its staff in preparation for an expected influx of
students at the close of the war. The board responded
within the limitations of available funds. By 1920 department heads were receiving from $2,250 to $2,750, depend-
ing upon training and experience. Averages in the College
of Agriculture, where federal funds were available, were
somewhat higher.

Another change instituted shortly after McVey became
President was a reorganization and expansion of the College of Arts and Sciences, which was undertaken in the
academic year 1918-1919. From this eventually resulted
an increase in the number of departments from thirteen
to twenty-two. Four new departments were created—
Health and Hygiene, Psychology, Music, and Art and
Design. Five more departments were gained by transfer,
Bacteriology, Botany, and Zoology from the College of
Agriculture, and two which had been considered as general
departments of the University, Military Science and Physical Education. The ROTC program, which was very young
when the war came on, was continued. An ample amount
of equipment was available, and for the first time a

[3] Minutes of Executive Committee, October 17, November 21, 1917,
February 19, 1919; Lexington *Leader*, December 17, 1917, July 7, 1918;
McVey Diary, January 14, 1944; Cooper to McVey, August 23, 1917,
McVey Papers; *Catalogue*, 1916-1917, p. 22, 1917-1918, p. 18, 1918-1919,
pp. 18, 21, 1919-1920, pp. 19-20, 25-26, 1920-1921, pp. 18, 22-23, 1921-
1922, pp. 24-25, 27, 1922-1923, pp. 16, 21, 23; Minutes of Board of
Trustees, December 10, 1917, December 10, 1918, April 1, 1919.

sufficient number of commissioned and noncommissioned officers were detailed as instructors. The new Department of Health and Hygiene consisted of three physicians and a trained nurse. President McVey considered the establishment of this department one of the major achievements in the early years of his administration. Various other administrative changes were made during these years. In accord with the recommendations of the Investigating Committee, the University's bookkeeping was centered in a single business office, and the financial records of the Experiment Station and the Department of Agricultural Extension were transferred to the Administration Building. A Practice High School was established in 1918, offering at first only two years of regular high school work and operating on a cooperative basis with the Lexington school system; by 1919 it offered a full four-year program and was operated solely by the University. Miss Frances Jewell, a graduate of Vassar, succeeded Miss Josephine Simrall as Dean of Women when Miss Simrall resigned after serving two years to take a similar position elsewhere.

While the University of Kentucky had begun to engage in Agricultural Extension under Barker, President McVey planned a broader program for taking the benefits of higher education to all the people of Kentucky who desired them. In addition to Agricultural Extension, a Department of University Extension was set up, supervised by a committee of which Dr. W. D. Funkhouser was chairman. Under the auspices of this new department, correspondence courses were made available both on the college and on the secondary level, and extension courses were taught, some at surprising distances from Lexington. By 1922 the annual enrollment in such courses had reached 500. Students were permitted to offer a total of thirty-two hours of extension or correspondence work toward graduation.

The Extension Department became a valuable link between the University and the high schools of Kentucky. Besides arranging for faculty members to speak before high school audiences as often as possible, this department inaugurated and sponsored debating contests in the secondary schools. In the spring, final tournaments were held on the University campus, attended by many members of teams already defeated. Hundreds of high school students, most of them above average in ability, received their first introduction to the University in this way.[4]

Agricultural Extension work also expanded, benefited by increasing federal support that was matched by state and local funds. Most of Kentucky's 120 counties soon had agricultural agents, who carried the findings of the Experiment Station and the teaching of the College of Agriculture to the farmer. Many counties also had home demonstration agents. The Department of Home Economics, which for a time had been operated independently, became a definite part of the College of Agriculture and moved into new quarters in the Agriculture Building. Under the Smith-Hughes program the University was also engaged in training teachers of agriculture, home economics, and other vocational subjects.

University faculty members were more active in national and regional organizations than they had been in the previous administration. President McVey set an example

4 Minutes of Board of Trustees, December 10, 1917, June 4, September 18, December 10, 1918, April 1, June 17, 1919, December 21, 1920, September 29, 1922; *Catalogue*, 1920-1921, p. 183; Lexington *Leader*, February 12, March 7, June 20, 1919, January 30, December 23, 1920; *The Kentucky Kernel*, March 8, 1921, June 2, 1922; Minutes of University Senate, February 10, 1919, November 8, 1920, January 10, 1921, October 9, 1922; Minutes of Executive Committee, January 9, November 22, 1918, January 15, June 23, September 10, 1919, July 7, 1920, May 4, 1921.

of such leadership. In 1920 he was elected president of the American Association for Agricultural Legislation. In 1922 he became president of the National Association of State Universities, and in the same year he was chosen to make a survey of higher education in Oklahoma. In 1919 Ezra Gillis became president of the American Association of College Registrars after serving for six years as its secretary. In 1921 Dean Cooper was elected president of the Association of Southern Agricultural Workers, Professor John J. Tigert was appointed to the position of United States Commissioner of Education, and Professor Funkhouser was named a Fellow of the Entomological Society of America.

An increased professional spirit was now found on the Lexington campus. A chapter of the American Association of University Professors was formed in 1919 with ten charter members, and in 1922 a chapter of Sigma Xi was installed, and to further this professional spirit, the administration stressed research and publication at every opportunity. In 1919 the Executive Committee established a fund for the publication of monographs, and in 1920 a Research Club was formed, consisting of those staff members who had made significant contributions in research and writing since leaving graduate school. One of the more notable scholars at this time was Dr. J. W. Pryor, head of the Department of Anatomy and Physiology and the first Kentucky scholar to become a member of the American Association of Anatomists. With an X-ray machine which he and Professor Merry L. Pence of the Physics Department had built, Pryor did pioneer work on the ossification of bones—work which is still recognized not only in America but in Europe as well. Though other faculty members were publishing, professors in the College of Agriculture, particularly those connected with the Experiment Station, led in published research. But the

University as a whole was still below standard in this aspect of scholarly activity.[5]

One hindrance to research was the library, which needed improvement both in quality and in quantity. Public appropriations came very slowly, and endowments by individuals were nonexistent. In 1917 the library had 33,869 volumes; by 1922 the number had increased to 48,483. Still the total could hardly be adequate for a university.

The University was already accredited by the Southern Association of Colleges and Secondary Schools, but now Dr. McVey sought to have it recognized by the Association of American Universities. While the University was not ready for membership in this exclusive organization, recognition by it would raise the school's standing both at home and abroad. The chairman of the Survey Commission of 1917, Dr. K. C. Babcock, was now chairman of the Association's Committee on the Classification of Universities and Colleges and was interested in what progress had been made in the University since the 1917 investigation. The association at its annual meeting in November, 1919, voted to place the University of Kentucky on its list of approved institutions. While this was not comparable to actual membership in the Association of American Universities, it did represent a considerable advance on the road toward maturity.

In its graduate program the school wisely concentrated upon the master's degree or its equivalent and made no

[5] Minutes of Executive Committee, March 26, 1919; *Catalogue, 1917-1918*, p. 81; Lexington *Leader*, December 12, 1919, January 11, 1920, February 17, 1921; Lexington *Herald*, December 17, 1918, February 19, 1921; *The Kentucky Kernel*, November 27, 1918, May 1, 1919, October 22, December 10, 1920, March 8, May 17, December 13, 1921, March 10, November 17, December 1, 1922; *University of Kentucky: Research Publications of Members of the Research Club* (Lexington, 1929), *passim;* Statement of Dr. John S. Chambers to author; Minutes of Board of Trustees, December 10, 1918, April 1, June 17, 1919, June 1, December 21, 1920, February 1, April 6, 1921, June 13, September 19, 1922.

attempt at this point to offer the doctorate. Graduate work was supervised by individual departments and coordinated by a graduate committee. A report in the fall of 1919 showed that Kentucky was one of only 130 institutions of higher learning in the United States whose graduate study was acceptable to the National Association of State Universities.[6]

Improvement of the physical plant of the University was limited in the early years of the McVey administration by rising prices and by a shortage of funds. When the county-appointee law was declared unconstitutional by the Kentucky Court of Appeals in 1917, the University converted the men's dormitories into classroom buildings. The "Old Dormitory" became White Hall and was used to house the Departments of Botany, Economics and Sociology, Art and Design, and Music. The "New Dormitory" was renamed Neville Hall and contained the Department of Hygiene and Public Health with its Dispensary, the Department of Bacteriology, and the Department of Psychology.

As housing off the campus, however, became increasingly more difficult to find at prices students could afford, the University began to build permanent dormitories for men in the style of the old Shaker buildings. The first of these new residence halls was completed in 1922 and would accommodate one hundred men. For the women, two large houses were rented and one was purchased for use as dormitories.

[6] Minutes of Board of Trustees, June 4, December 10, 1918, June 17, 1919, September 19, November 24, 1922; Lexington *Leader*, November 10, 1922; Lexington *Herald*, February 19, 1921, March 19, 1922; Louisville *Courier-Journal*, March 19, 1922; *The Kentucky Kernel*, November 21, 1919; Lawrence S. Thompson, "Books at the University of Kentucky," *Filson Club History Quarterly*, XXIV (1950), 65; McVey to H. V. Ames, February 11, 1919, Ames to McVey, February 14, 1919, Kendric C. Babcock to McVey, February 17, 1919, McVey to Babcock, February 25, 1919, Babcock to McVey, April 25, 1919, David A. Robertson to McVey, December 9, 1919, McVey Papers.

The first floor of the Administration Building was remodeled, and here were located the offices of the President, the Dean of Men, the Dean of the College of Arts and Sciences, the business agent, the registrar, the superintendent of buildings and grounds, and the Stenographic Bureau. In 1919 a bookstore and a post office were opened in the basement of the Administration Building.[7]

One of the recommendations of the 1917 Investigating Committee had been the formation and adoption of a constitution defining the functions of the board and of the faculty, and a document consisting of two parts, one called "Rules and Regulations of the Board of Trustees of the University of Kentucky" and the other called "Governing Regulations," was adopted by the board on December 10, 1917, shortly after McVey became President. It described the President as "the expert adviser of the Board of Trustees and chief executive officer of the University." He was to be "elected for an indefinite period" and to "hold office during good behavior and satisfactory service."

There was to be a Council consisting of the President, "the deans of the colleges, the chairman of the Graduate School Committee, the Dean of Men, the Dean of Women, the Registrar (secretary ex officio), the director of the Experiment Station, the Director of Extension, together with two members elected annually by the Senate." The Council would administer the regulations established by the Senate but would have no legislative functions. It was also given "exclusive and final jurisdiction over all

7 Minutes of Board of Trustees, December 10, 1917, June 4, September 18, December 10, 1918, April 1, June 17, September 16, 1919, September 21, 1920, April 6, October 5, 1921, April 4, June 13, September 19, November 23, 1922; *The Kentucky Kernel,* January 23, March 27, September 26, 1919, March 26, December 7, 1920, November 4, 1921, April 20, 1922; Lexington *Leader,* March 3, 1918, February 10, June 13, 1919; Minutes of Executive Committee, July 17, 1918, July 23, September 10, 1919, June 1, July 7, 1920, March 8, 1922, July 20, 1923.

cases of discipline," and it was responsible for making decisions regarding scholarships and attendance.

The Senate was the legislative body of the University. It was composed of the members of the Council, except for the chairman of the Graduate School Committee who was replaced by the librarian, and all professors, associate professors, and assistant professors. It was given "jurisdiction over all matters involving general University policy, so far as these are not reserved to the Board of Trustees or to the President." It was expected to make "such rules and regulations as it may deem advisable to promote the educational interests of the University."

The Assembly consisted of all who were members of the Senate plus instructors and personnel engaged in state service work. It might "formulate its attitude upon any matter affecting the institution" and could make recommendations to the Senate, the Council, the President, or the Board of Trustees.

The suggestion of the Investigating Committee that the size of the Board of Trustees be reduced from thirty-two to fifteen was enacted by the legislature in 1918. The new board had three ex officio members, the Governor, the Superintendent of Public Instruction, and the Commissioner of Agriculture. The other twelve members were to be appointed by the Governor, four each biennium for six-year terms. One of the four was to be a member of the State Board of Agriculture, one an alumnus of the University selected by the Governor from a group of three nominated by the alumni, and the other two were to be "distinguished citizens of the Commonwealth," one from each of the two major political parties.

One final administrative change to be made as a result of the work of the Survey Commission and the Investigating Committee concerned the engineering colleges. After considering this problem for a year, McVey recommended in September, 1918, that the three engineering colleges be combined into one College of Engineering with F. Paul Anderson as its dean. The Board of Trustees adopted this plan without a dissenting vote and thus disposed of one of the major points of controversy carried over from the Barker administration.

This postwar period extending into the early twenties was a time when public relations were unusually important, for the administration was anxious that the people of the state know more about their University. President McVey gave many talks before civic clubs, the YMCA and various community organizations. The Department of Music sent its glee club on tours of the state, had its band appear before the legislature, and sponsored orchestra concerts which were open to the public. Essay contests among high school students were encouraged, and women's clubs, schools, and community organizations were given assistance by the University in the presentation of plays and pageants. High school basketball tournaments were held on the campus and may have encouraged boys in regard to higher education and in favor of their own state University. Dr. C. B. Cornell of the Psychology Department gave a great deal of time to administering intelligence tests in the public schools and in various state institutions. The ever-popular Farmers' Week held in January of each year was continued and expanded.

Another effort to acquaint citizens of the state with the University was made in 1921 when the Board of Trustees asked a number of interested citizens to make a tour of inspection of publicly supported universities in Ohio, Indiana, Illinois, and Wisconsin. The travelers saw the physical plants of these schools, all superior to that of the University of Kentucky, and gathered figures on the support they received from their respective states. They were told, for one thing, that proper instruction and demonstration in agriculture required at least 1,000 acres of land. Kentucky had only 240 acres. "The inadequacy of the [Kentucky] herds, flocks, and studs for the work in animal husbandry," they reported on their return, "is more than marked; it is astonishing. Substantial expenditures should be made in this direction at once." They recommended also the establishment of experimental substations for investigating farm problems that could not be successfully worked out at Lexington. The report was not entirely pessimistic. The commission found that the personnel of the University of Kentucky was well known and was respected in the educational field of which it was a part.

Slow progress was also being made in the University's financial support from the state. In the fiscal year 1918-1919 the total income of the University, including federal funds and fees collected, passed the million dollar mark for the first time. For the 1920-1922 biennium the state contributed about $1,400,000 toward a total income of slightly more than $2,500,000. But in the next biennium, even after the sobering report of the group which had investigated state institutions in the Midwest, the legislature appropriated only $1,495,818, the sum remaining after an executive veto had removed $290,000.[8]

In 1920 an Athletic Council was formed and made responsible for the management of the athletic program. It consisted of the President, the Director of Athletics, the treasurer of the Athletic Association, three members of the teaching staff, appointed by the President, three alumni or interested citizens residing in Fayette County, also selected by the President, and two students, either

[8] Kentucky General Assembly *Acts*, 1918, p. 127; Minutes of University Senate, November 17, 1919; *The University of Kentucky: Its History and Development*, p. 30; Lexington *Herald*, December 6, 1917, April 2, 1919; Lexington *Leader*, February 1, 1918, March 4, October 10, December 22, 1919, February 6, 1920, February 26, 1922; *The Kentucky Kernel*, March 7, 1918, March 20, 1919, March 19, 1920, March 31, 1922; Minutes of Board of Trustees, December 10, 1917, June 4, September 18, December 18, 1918, June 17, 1919, June 13, 1921, April 4, 1922.

named by the President or selected by the student body in a manner designated by him.

In 1921 Kentucky joined with fifteen other members of the Southern Intercollegiate Athletic Association in the forming of a new athletic organization called the Southern Intercollegiate Conference. The word "Intercollegiate" was dropped from the name in 1923. This conference was made up primarily of state universities and land grant colleges, although a few of the larger private schools were accepted. The Southern started as a football conference, and as late as 1924 Kentucky was still playing basketball as a member of the SIAA. The school's first participation in a Southern Conference basketball tournament was in 1925.

Student life during the early years of McVey's presidency began to lose some of the rowdiness which had been characteristic of former days. McVey's own personality may have been in part responsible for this change. Though a warm person with a fine sense of humor, his dignified and even austere appearance contrasted with the heartiness of former President Barker. The tug of war between the freshmen and the sophomores, which had not been held during the war, was resumed, but it was no longer marked by the violence which had once accompanied it, and the practice of hazing was gradually dying out. In the cultural life of the campus the literary societies were still active, and the Strollers continued to present plays at the Lexington Opera House, while a number of notable artists gave performances at the city's Woodland Auditorium.[9]

9 *The Kentucky Kernel*, February 14, April 11, 1918, April 3, May 8, 15, September 26, 1919, January 23, March 5, 12, April 2, 16, 23, May 21, November 5, 12, 1920, March 1, 22, April 5, 15, November 21, 1921, January 13, March 10, 17, April 28, November 24, December 15, 1922, December 14, 1923; Lexington *Leader*, October 16, 1917; Minutes of Council, February 13, 1922; Minutes of University Senate, March 8, 1920, February 14, 1921.

In February, 1921, the University Senate accepted a recommendation of the Discipline Committee to the effect that if there were a real desire expressed on the part of the student body for a representative council which would act under faculty supervision, as was the custom in many institutions, the faculty would be ready to cooperate. In April a student was sent to a conference on student government held at the University of Missouri. After his return a constitution was drawn up. A Men's Student Council was created consisting of four seniors, three juniors, two sophomores, and one freshman. Its duties were more social than disciplinary; it scheduled dances and other student activities and also supervised the annual elections of class officers. The women students, many of whom lived in campus dormitories, had for several years operated a Women's Self-Government Association effectively. In the President's report to the Board in 1922 he said that student government among the men had been working well. At first the council wanted more authority than it had been given, but when its members realized that greater authority would require a greater measure of responsibility on their part, they were content to let things remain as they were.[10]

In 1922 occurred the death of President Emeritus Patterson. Mindful of the school which he had worked so hard to build, Patterson bequeathed his property to the University, including a valuable library of books, later placed in the University library as a special collection.

The five years from 1917 to 1922 differed noticeably from the preceding five years. While the work of the

[10] Minutes of University Senate, January 17, 1918, February 14, 1921; Minutes of Board of Trustees, June 1, 1920, June 13, 1922; Lexington *Leader*, September 11, 1917, September 18, 1918, May 15, 16, 18, 20, 1919, November 9, 10, 1920; *The Kentucky Kernel*, November 1, 1917, May 22, October 24, 1919, October 15, 1920, April 15, May 10, 20, October 7, 1921, April 28, 1922.

Investigating Committee and the Survey Commission was felt both in ending certain unwise practices and in suggesting improvements, there were certainly other factors that were highly effective in reshaping the life of the University.

In place of the divisive jealousies that tended to divert directors from their constructive work, this period was marked by the fine leadership of such faculty members as William D. Funkhouser, Thomas P. Cooper, Edward Wiest, J. W. Pryor, and C. B. Cornell, to mention but a few. It was also characterized by increased efforts to take the University to the people of Kentucky and by the increase of members of the teaching staff who held Ph.D.'s, who belonged to professional societies, who held some office in a national organization, or who were publishing the results of their scholarly work. It was a mark of this improvement when the University was accredited by the Association of American Universities, even though it was not yet a member. To be sure, the University continued to be inadequately financed, but already the leadership of President McVey was proving its worth, not only among the faculty but among the students as well.

CHAPTER VI

NEW COLLEGES AND DEPARTMENTS

DURING the five years from 1922 to 1927 the institution
continued to grow, although slowly, and to assume more
and more the structure of a true university. New colleges
and departments were created, and the University's income slowly increased, though not in keeping with the
growth of enrollments. Much, however, remained the
same. The responsibilities of the deans was little altered.
Among the students, the Strollers continued to entertain
with their plays, the athletic teams continued their rather
mediocre record, and rivalry between freshmen and sophomores went on, though with new tricks. Most significantly,
the state's traditional reluctance to support wholeheartedly
its institution of higher education was still evident, as
could be seen in the defeat of a bond issue in 1924, part
of which would have gone to the University.

The growth of the University and the spread of its
influence within the state made it a natural target for
pressures of various kinds. One of the more serious of
these attacks was the controversy over the teaching of
evolution, which reached its climax in Kentucky some
three years before the famous Scopes trial in Tennessee.
The University had made no secret of its acceptance of
current scientific knowledge of the development of man
and of the age of the earth. In the spring of 1919 Dean
Boyd arranged for an interdisciplinary course in organic
evolution to be offered as an elective for all the sciences.
The next fall this course was expanded to three hours a
week and included lecturers from the Departments of
Psychology and Philosophy.

The first apparent protest against the University's teaching appeared in the summer of 1921 in a letter to the Louisville *Evening Post* from a man in Elizabethtown, who wrote that he would oppose any financial aid to the school if the reports of Darwinian theories being taught there were true. Later a Baptist publication picked up the charge that the University was permeated by materialism and evolutionary doctrines. In December of the same year a more concerted move was made by the Baptist State Board of Missions; at its meeting in Louisville a resolution was introduced charging that not only the University but also many of the high schools were engaged in teaching the degrading notions of Darwin. As a result of this resolution, a committee was appointed to draw up a campaign against evolution, and one of its members was to look into the funds going to the University if it did not conform to the committee's demands.

When the General Assembly met in January of 1922, two bills against evolution were introduced, one in the House by G. W. Ellis and the other in the Senate by J. R. Rash. The House bill, the more stringent of the two, provided for a fine with the possibilities of a jail sentence and the loss of an institution's charter.

Support for the University was offered by two Louisville papers, the *Evening Post* and the *Courier-Journal*. The pastors of the some of the Lexington churches spoke out in favor of the stand taken by the University, and President E. Y. Mullins of the Southern Baptist Theological Seminary commended McVey's statement of the University's position, which was released on February 12. In defending his cause, McVey secured statements from a number of prominent educators in the country, and he received private encouragement from George Colvin, the Superintendent of Public Instruction for the state. The leading figure who spoke for the antievolutionists was William

Jennings Bryan, who gave addresses in Danville, Paris, and Lexington and before a joint meeting of the legislature in Frankfort. On March 9, 1922, the House debated the Ellis bill for five hours. When the vote was taken, the bill was defeated by a vote of only 42 to 41. In the Senate the Rash bill died in committee. No similar bills were introduced in Kentucky until 1926, and these never came to a vote. Thus ended one of the threats to the University's freedom, but other lesser and sometimes more subtle ones would come in the future.[1]

While the evolution controversy was in progress, plans were being made for the added growth of the University. The Survey Commission of 1917 had recommended that the Department of Education be expanded into a college, and a similar recommendation had been made by an Educational Commission created by the 1920 legislature. But at that time there had not been sufficient funds to carry out these recommendations.

By the spring of 1923, however, newspapers were speculating that a college would soon be created and that George Colvin, State Superintendent of Public Instruction and ex officio member of the Board of Trustees, would become dean. There were even rumors that a Covington politician had offered to make Colvin dean if he would not seek the Republican nomination for Governor. Several

[1] Kentucky Kernel, February 6, October 3, 1919; Louisville Evening Post, July 14, 1921; Louisville Courier-Journal, December 8, 1921; McVey to Editor of Western Recorder, September 19, 1921, McVey Papers; Copies of Ellis Bill and Rash Bill, McVey Papers; Norman F. Furniss, The Fundamentalist Controversy, 1918-1931 (New Haven, 1954), pp. 80-83; Frank L. McVey, The Gates Open Slowly (Lexington, 1949), pp. 221-36, 292-96; Lexington Leader, December 7, 1921, January 19, 23, 1922; Lexington Herald, January 23, April 20, 1922; Louisville Times, January 26, 1922; Mrs. Charles F. Norton to Governor Edwin P. Morrow, January 23, 1922, copy, McVey Papers; McVey's telegram, the replies, and newspaper clippings on the subject, McVey Papers; Minutes of Executive Committee, June 1, 1922.

members of the board denied that they were being sub-
jected to any such political pressure, though one trustee
did admit that Colvin's name had been mentioned in this
connection in meetings of the Executive Committee.

On May 22, 1923, part of the rumor was confirmed
when President McVey recommended that a College of
Education be established. Its nucleus would be the existing Departments of Education and Vocational Teacher
Training. The board approved the recommendation, but
Colvin did not become dean. Instead, the board accepted
McVey's choice of William S. Taylor. Taylor had received
the degree of Bachelor of Science in Agriculture in 1912
from the University. In 1913 he had earned the degree of
Master of Science at the University of Wisconsin. At the
time of his appointment he had completed the requirements for the degree of Doctor of Philosophy at Columbia,
and the degree was awarded in June, 1923. He had taught
at the University of Texas, at the State College of Pennsylvania, and had headed a bureau in Pennsylvania's
Department of Education.

The College of Education in the University of Kentucky
opened in the fall of 1923. It was authorized to grant
both the A.B. and B.S. degrees as well as the M.A. and the
M.S. It had four departments—Educational Administration and Supervision, Educational Psychology, History
and Philosophy of Education, and Principles and Practice
of Education—with most of the work offered by Dean
Taylor, Professor Cotton Noe, Professor Moses E. Ligon,
who served also as the Principal of the University High
School, and Assistant Professor Wellington Patrick. Courses
in agricultural education, in home economics education,
and in industrial education were taught by specialists in
those fields. Methods of teaching art, botany, English, and
mathematics were first offered by the respective departments, but in the fall of 1925 they were shifted to teachers

in the University High School. By 1925 most of the work in agricultural education was being handled by Assistant Professor Carsie Hammonds, who eventually became head of that department and played a major role in its development. Specific training for elementary school teachers was first offered in 1926.

Gradually the staff of the college was enlarged by the addition of Dr. Jesse E. Adams, Dr. Clay C. Ross, Dr. Floyd W. Reeves, John Dale Russell, and Ralph H. Woods. Adams devoted most of his time to philosophy of education, Ross took over educational psychology, and Reeves became Director of the Bureau of Educational Service. After serving as Superintendent of Public Instruction in the administration of Governor Fields, McHenry Rhoads returned to the University as professor of secondary education.

President McVey, in 1924, also recommended that a College of Commerce be established, and the Board of Trustees approved. According to McVey's plan, the new college with Dr. Edward Wiest as dean would take over courses in economics, business administration, and secretarial work, formerly offered in the Department of Economics and Sociology. Located in White Hall, the new college formally began in the fall of 1925, with authority to grant a B.S. degree.

A part of the University which received fresh impetus during this period was the Graduate School. Actually, after the resignation of Alexander S. Mackenzie in 1916, this area languished, with graduate work supervised by a committee. Early in 1924 the President recommended that the Graduate School be reorganized and that a dean be appointed, and at the beginning of the next year Dr. Funkhouser was named dean.

At the end of the 1924-1925 school year McVey reported to the Board of Trustees that seventy-four graduate students had been enrolled during the regular term and that the additional number enrolled in the summer session would bring the figure close to one hundred. A year later there were 125 graduate students, 35 of whom would receive master's degrees in June, 1926.

Graduate work increased to such an extent that the question of offering the Ph.D. in some departments was considered. In September, 1926, it was recommended that work leading to the doctorate be started in departments with the required staff and facilities, as determined by the President and the Dean of the Graduate School and confirmed by the University Senate, and the program was to begin the following year. The first departments to offer the doctorate were Chemistry, Economics, Education, Mathematics, Physics, and Psychology.

This expansion of the graduate program brought a great increase in the number of graduate students. Many Kentuckians who formerly would have gone to other states for their graduate work now came to the University, and a considerable number were attracted from outside the state. The offering of the doctoral degree in several fields led some, who otherwise would have started their graduate work elsewhere, to work at Kentucky from the beginning. In 1926-1927, 157 graduate students were enrolled; and by 1927-1928 the number reached 564.[2]

In addition to staff increases brought about by the founding of new colleges, several other changes occurred in the faculty during the middle twenties. After the death of Dean W. T. Lafferty of the College of Law, Charles J. Turck was selected in the spring of 1924 as dean of this

2 Frank L. McVey, *The Gates Open Slowly* (Lexington, 1949), p. 188; *The University of Kentucky: Its History and Development*, p. 21; Minutes of University Senate, April 6, May 28, 1925, March 14, 1927; Minutes of Executive Committee, May 22, 1923, January 21, 1924; Minutes of Board of Trustees, April 4, 1922, June 12, October 2, 1923, April 7, May 30, 1925, May 29, September 28, 1926.

college. Only thirty-four at the time of his appointment, Turck held both M.A. and LL.B. degrees from Columbia. In addition to practicing law with a New York firm, he had been a professor of law at both Tulane and Vanderbilt universities. Turck remained as Dean of the College of Law for three years, leaving in 1927 to accept the presidency of Centre College. During his tenure as dean the College of Law was first given a Class A rating by the American Bar Association. His successor was Alvin Evans from George Washington University.

Another change in personnel of the University occurred in the fall of 1923 when the Dean of Women, Frances Jewell, resigned to become the second wife of President McVey, whose first wife had died early in 1922. Miss Sarah G. Blanding, a recent graduate of the University and an assistant to Dean Jewell, was named as acting dean. After a leave of absence for graduate study, she returned to the University in 1925 as Dean of Women and assistant professor of political science.

In the College of Arts and Sciences two new departments were set up during the mid-twenties. Political Science, which had been combined with History, became a separate department in 1926. As a result of the explorations and excavations of Dr. Funkhouser and Professor W. S. Webb, head of the Department of Physics, who had been spending their vacations studying the prehistoric peoples of Kentucky, the Board of Trustees created a Department of Anthropology and Archeology in July, 1927. Funkhouser and Webb were named professors in the new department with no additional salary.[3]

The University continued to make every possible effort

[3] Minutes of Board of Trustees, June 12, 1923, April 4, 1924, May 30, 1925, April 13, 1926, May 28, 1927; Minutes of Executive Committee, July 20, November 21, 1923, July 27, 1927; *Kentucky Kernel*, November 16, 23, 1923, January 11, 1924, September 25, 1925, February 11, 25, April 22, July 8, 1927.

to serve those who could not attend during the regular academic year or who could be helped by short courses or meetings. The Extension Department increased its offerings, and the summer term was lengthened. By 1927 the summer session enrollment had passed thirteen hundred. The Farm and Home Week, held in January of each year, attracted increasing numbers of farmers and their wives. It was estimated that the College of Agriculture through its extension workers came into direct contact with one-third of the people of Kentucky each year. In 1924 Ezra Gillis, who had been active in the American Association of College Registrars, started at the University of Kentucky an institute for the training of registrars. Its second session, held in April, 1925, was attended by persons from thirty-six different institutions. The Colleges of Education and of Commerce both set up departments to serve the state in 1927. The Bureau of Educational Service, later known as the Bureau of School Service, made the facilities of the College of Education available to the schools of the state in solving their problems. The Bureau of Business Research, which began operating at the beginning of the 1928-1929 school year, offered the services of the College of Commerce to business in the state.[4]

Under the supervision of Miss Margaret I. King the library grew from 53,746 volumes in 1923 to 77,332 volumes in 1927. The librarian was faced with two problems, lack of money and lack of space. The library building, which was adequate when built in 1909, did not begin to meet the needs of 1927.

[4] *Kentucky Kernel,* March 2, December 14, 1923, February 8, November 28, 1924, January 23, March 20, May 1, 8, September 25, October 2, 1925, January 8, 15, May 7, 1926, February 4, July 1, August 19, December 29, 1927; Minutes of Board of Trustees, June 12, 1923, May 30, 1925, May 28, December 20, 1927; Minutes of Executive Committee, March 28, 1923, February 10, 1925, June 23, July 21, 1926, June 21, 1927.

In the decade of the twenties a little more than half of the University's income came from the state. The remainder came primarily from the federal government, which provided a considerable part of the support for Agricultural Extension and the Experiment Station, from fees, and from restricted funds—money contributed by a foundation, a corporation, or an individual. Restricted funds usually were given for specified purposes, and normally only the interest could be used.

For the 1922-1924 biennium the University received from the state $1,495,818, out of a total income of $2,675,944. When the legislature met in 1924, Governor William J. Fields presented a plan for a $75,000,000 bond issue, the money to be used for the building of roads and for the improvement and expansion of the state's institutions, including its schools. Of this amount $5,000,000 was to be made available to the University. The plan was passed by both houses subject to a popular referendum on November 4. In spite of efforts made by the University and by groups of civic-minded people, the bond issue was defeated by a large margin.

The legislature, however, had not left the University entirely dependent upon the success or failure of the bond plan. A new inheritance tax law had been passed, and one of its provisions was that one-fourth of the money raised in this way would go to the University. It was expected that this 25 percent would bring about $75,000 annually to the school. The Nelson Tax Act, passed at the same session, reapportioned the money obtained from the tax on intangibles, and the University was to receive 2.01 cents out of every 30 cents collected. For the 1924-1926 biennium the school's total income was $3,248,513, of which $1,818,597 came from the state.

In 1925 Congress passed the Purnell Act to enable the agricultural experiment stations to do more work in the fields of rural economics, rural sociology, and home economics. It gave to each station $20,000 for the first year, with an annual increase of $10,000 until the amount reached $60,000 per year. These sums did not have to be matched by the state, but the states were required to accept officially the terms of the act. This the Kentucky General Assembly did in 1926.

At this session another bond issue was attempted. This called for $5,000,000 for educational purposes, and of this amount $4,600,000 would go to the University. This was passed by the House of Representatives, but certain changes made by the Senate were not acceptable to the lower house, and upon its return it was defeated by a narrow margin. The 1926 session of the legislature did appropriate $150,000 for the construction of a women's dormitory and changed the inheritance tax law to allow the University 50 percent instead of only 25 percent of the income derived from this source. During the 1926-1928 biennium the state gave the University $2,572,758 of its total income of $4,362,109.

The University's increase in enrollment between 1923 and 1927, while not spectacular, was sufficient to overtax its classrooms, library, and laboratory facilities. Enrollment grew from 1,752 students in 1922-1923 to 2,485 in 1926-1927. McVey attributed this growth to the ever-increasing number of students graduating from Kentucky high schools. On this basis he predicted an enrollment of 3,500 by 1930. "Unless some relief comes in the way of additional funds," he told the Board of Trustees, "we shall be compelled to limit the number of students admitted to the institution."

In October, 1923, McVey listed among the needs of the University a classroom building for the College of Arts and Sciences, additional library space, another Agriculture building, an addition to the Engineering group to take care of the equipment promised by industrialist, Henry Wendt, and a larger cafeteria.

During the five years from 1922 to 1927 a number of buildings were added to the campus. Kastle Hall was completed; a new dormitory for girls was built south of Patterson Hall in 1925, later named Boyd Hall. The Henry W. Wendt Shop of the College of Engineering was completed in 1927 and housed the machinery donated by Wendt. In 1923 a group of students converted a former Negro church on Winslow Street (now Euclid Avenue) into a little theater which became known as the Romany. By 1927 the University had enlarged this building sufficiently to house the Departments of Art and Music as well.

Although the teaching day was lengthened from seven to eight periods in an effort to solve the problem of over-crowded classrooms, this was not sufficient. And by the spring of 1927 plans were being drawn for a building to house the Departments of English, Mathematics, Journalism, and a cafeteria. It was to be located west of Kastle Hall, and work on it was started in the fall of that year. The Board of Trustees, over McVey's protest, voted to name it in his honor.[5]

In the meantime a structure less essential but more popular in nature was built on the campus. The campaign for funds with which to construct a War Memorial Building had bogged down with about $80,000 collected. The plan at first was to use these funds toward constructing

[5] Minutes of Executive Committee, July 2, 1924, March 11, November 11, 1925, January 12, March 17, June 23, November 12, 1926; Minutes of Board of Trustees, October 2, 1923, April 4, 1924, May 30, 1925, April 13, 1926, April 5, May 28, December 20, 1927; *Kentucky Kernel,* July 20, October 5, 1923, March 28, November 7, 1924, January 8, March 19, October 29, 1926, May 28, September 23, 1927; Louisville *Courier-Journal,* January 9, 1924; Thompson, "Books at the University of Kentucky," 65; *The University of Kentucky: Its History and Development,* pp. 22, 30-31.

a new stadium. On March 28, 1923, however, Dr. Funkhouser and some other members of the Athletic Council appeared before the Executive Committee of the Board to request the construction of a new gymnasium. They pointed out that the present gymnasium was unsafe even for the small number of people it could accommodate, that large crowds had to be turned away, and that the popular state high school basketball tournament might be moved to Louisville if the University did not provide better facilities.

The Board approved the plan for a gymnasium, and the Alumni Association immediately started to raise funds for the building, which would be on Winslow Street west of Stoll Field. The gymnasium was completed in 1924 at a cost of $110,000. Of this amount, $70,000 was contributed by the Alumni Association. It was expected that $30,000 of the $40,000 advanced by the University would be repaid by receipts from games. In addition to serving for basketball, the new building could be used as an auditorium, making it possible to convert the old chapel in the Administration Building into a reading room supervised by the library staff. Physical education classes for men were moved into the Alumni Gymnasium, and the old gymnasium was turned over to the women's physical education work. In addition to locker rooms, the basement of the Alumni Gymnasium housed the University Post Office and Book Store.

While the gymnasium was under construction, a concrete stadium was being erected at the opposite end of Stoll Field. The University of Kentucky Stadium Fund, created by the Alumni Association, borrowed $50,000 from the Memorial Building Fund at 6 percent and raised the remaining $70,000 by public subscription. The stadium was dedicated on November 1, 1924. The two stands of three sections each would seat a total of about ten thousand people. It was expected at the time that eight more sections would eventually be added, making a U-shaped stadium seating 25,000.

The decade of the 1920's saw a great increase in the University's land holdings. The Experiment Station Farm in Lexington was enlarged by 233 acres through the purchase of two adjacent farms. In eastern Kentucky an Agricultural Experiment Substation was established at Quicksand in Breathitt County on a large tract of land deeded to the University by the E. O. Robinson Foundation. In western Kentucky the people of Caldwell County purchased a tract near Princeton and deeded it to the University with the understanding that an Experiment Substation would be established there. The General Assembly appropriated funds for the maintenance of both of these stations, and they were dedicated in September, 1925, both having since made valuable contributions to the people of their areas.[6]

The administrative organization of the University which was planned and adopted soon after McVey's arrival continued with little change. In December, 1923, the University Senate approved a petition from the Men's Student Council asking that that body be allowed a representative on the Discipline Committee and in the Senate itself. In March, 1924, a similar request from the Women's Administrative Council was approved.

In the spring of 1925 the President in his report to the Board of Trustees mentioned that there was a growing belief that institutions had obligations to their students which could not be met in the classroom. He referred in

[6] Minutes of Board of Trustees, April 13, June 12, October 2, 1923, April 4, May 31, September 23, December 9, 1924, April 5, 1927; Minutes of Executive Committee, March 28, July 20, September 26, 1923, February 16, March 7, November 14, 1924, February 10, 1925, May 17, June 23, 1926; Kentucky General Assembly *Acts*, 1924, pp. 2-4; *Kentucky Kernel*, September 28, 1923, November 21, 1924, September 25, October 2, 1925.

particular to the need for helping students with their personal problems, whether they were social, moral, or economic. At the University of Kentucky there had been a steady increase in the number of people engaged in instruction, but the growth of the administrative staffs had been very slight. "Everywhere expansion has taken place," he said, "except in the President's office or that of the Deans."

No recommendations were made at the time, but the following year an Office of Publicity and Alumni Affairs was created. It was not until 1927, however, that the organization of a Personnel Bureau was proposed by the President, and approved by the board. This bureau did not go into full operation until 1930.

The pattern of social life on the campus continued apparently little changed from preceding years. The city of Lexington and the surrounding countryside was largely agricultural, and events there moved at a slow, even tempo. The students, though, appeared to be acquiring a more sophisticated attitude, as instanced in the virtual absence of hazing and of rowdy celebrations. With the gradual lapsing of these earlier, essentially masculine, amusements, there was a corresponding growth in social organizations for the students. During the five-year period covered by this chapter four new fraternities and three sororities established chapters on the campus, and a number of honorary groups, including ones in law, mathematics, and journalism as well as Phi Beta Kappa and Omicron Delta Kappa, appeared on the campus for the first time. Athletics were always popular, but the improved facilities which the University provided for them during these five years did not effect a corresponding improvement in the records of University teams. Football made the poorer showing, with a record of nineteen wins, twenty-three losses, and four ties for the period, while the basketball teams did a little better, winning forty-seven games and losing thirty-seven. That violence had not entirely died out was dramatically revealed by a pistol duel that took place in February, 1923. A nightwatchman was killed and a student seriously wounded in this encounter, which resulted in a plea from President McVey for all students with weapons to turn them in to the University.[7]

From 1922 to 1927 the University of Kentucky continued to grow as circumstances demanded. New colleges and new departments were added. Income and buildings increased, but not in the same proportion as the enrollment. A good indication of the conservative temper of the state was the close vote in the General Assembly on the controversy over evolution. It is interesting to note that the University apparently did not share in the exuberance which is associated with the mid-twenties. But, then, like the rest of the country, it also had no forebodings of what the next decade would bring.

[7] *Kentucky Kernel,* 1923-1927, *passim;* Louisville *Courier-Journal,* February 12, 13, 14, 15, 1923; Minutes of University Senate, December 17, 1923, March 10, 1924, April 26, 1926, May 27, 1927; Minutes of Board of Trustees, May 30, 1925, May 29, 1926, May 28, 1927.

CHAPTER VII

DEPTHS OF THE DEPRESSION

THE DEPRESSION of the early thirties did not come upon the University suddenly. To primarily agricultural Kentucky the financial crash of 1929 was muted. Around 1930 the University enjoyed a considerable building program, but only a little later the effects of the depression were felt in the reduced income of the school and in the consequent reductions in salaries for the staff. Enrollment, however, continued to rise.

The period from 1928 to 1932 saw a considerable expansion of the University. Ten new buildings were added on the main campus, but some of these were small, like the Observatory, built to replace an older one, and the Small-Animal House where animals used for experimental work were kept.

McVey Hall, the University's largest and finest classroom building at the time, was completed in 1928. Containing three floors, a basement, and at its south end a subbasement, it served many purposes. On the first floor were the classrooms and offices of the Department of Mathematics plus a large lecture room used by various departments. On the second floor were the classrooms and offices of the Department of English. The third floor had a faculty clubroom at one end, and in the rest of the space was a large cafeteria, the University Commons.

A sidelight on the depression at the University is given by the elevator in McVey Hall that ran from the subbasement to the cafeteria kitchen. It was intended solely for deliveries and for use by cafeteria personnel, and a sign warned others not to use it. When the depression came in the early thirties, the cafeteria's business declined. Some students skipped at least one meal a day or made a lunch of a pint of milk and three sweet rolls which could be bought just across Limestone Street from the campus for only ten cents. The sign on the elevator came down, and nothing was said if students used it to reach the cafeteria. As the depression deepened, the cafeteria management, still trying to furnish an adequate diet, was hard pushed to make ends meet. Now a sign went up directing faculty and students to the elevator and urging them to use it.

The basement of McVey Hall was occupied by the Department of Journalism, the Kernel Press, the Campus Book Store, and the University Post Office. The latter two had been badly in need of a new location, for in the summer of 1928 their quarters in the basement of the new gymnasium had been visited by two floods in quick succession. Losses exceeded $20,000, and in the fall of the same year a fire originating in the gymnasium boilerroom adjoining the Post Office had done additional damage. Shortly after the bookstore moved into its new quarters, the University transferred its operation to James E. Morris on a contract basis. Under the contract the University would furnish the space and receive a share of the profits.

For many years a campaign had been carried on throughout the state for funds with which to erect a building to serve as a memorial to those Kentuckians who gave their lives in the World War. Contributions came in sporadically, and at one time consideration was given to using these funds in building a gymnasium and a stadium, a plan which came to nothing. Finally it was decided that an auditorium would be built. It may not have been the University's greatest need, but at least it was a need. The auditorium, which came to be known as Memorial Hall, was dedicated on Memorial Day, 1929, with Under

Secretary of War Patrick J. Hurley as the principal speaker. With its Corinthian columns and its tall spire, it was the most beautiful building that had been erected on the campus up to this time. At the rear of the building a semicircular amphitheater was constructed that was used for concerts, motion pictures, and other programs during the warm months. An excellent pipe organ was installed in the building and was used by both local and visiting artists and by the Department of Music.

After the Department of Education became a college, it soon outgrew its quarters, for the Education Building was shared by the college and the University High School. Space for an elementary school was badly needed so that those who expected to teach on that level could be properly trained. As it seemed unlikely that the state would supply enough money for an adequate building, in 1927 an application was made to the General Education Board for a grant. The University would furnish the land, provide the equipment, maintain the building, and make annual provision for operation of the school. The response was favorable. The foundation agreed to give $150,000 toward the erection of a Training School Building if the University would provide an equal amount.

A site across Limestone Street from the main campus, a former city dump that had been filled and named Scovell Park, was deeded to the Board of Trustees of the University as a site for the new building, and work on the $300,000 structure was started early in 1929. It consisted of three parts; the middle portion housed the College of Education, the left wing the University High School, and the right wing the University Elementary School. Its two acres of floor space included not only classrooms and offices, but also an auditorium, a gymnasium, a cafeteria, and a library. The new building was occupied in the fall of 1930.

The only dormitory for men on the campus at the time was located parallel to Rose Street just north of Washington Avenue and had been completed in 1922. The legislature in 1928 passed a measure permitting the erection of dormitories on the amortization plan. By the end of the year two had been started. One was located parallel to the 1922 building and was almost identical in outward appearance. Instead of having long corridors running the full length of each of its four floors, however, it was divided into three sections to reduce the amount of noise and to be more conducive to study. The third dormitory was constructed facing Washington Avenue, at right angles to the other two so that the three together formed a U. Similar in size and architecture, it was the most elaborate of the three, with tall columns three stories high on the front. The new buildings were first occupied in the fall of 1929.

The two new dormitories were paid for not by the state but through rental charged the students. The University deeded the land on which they stand to the Security Trust Company of Lexington. The trust company then contracted with the Combs Lumber Company to construct the buildings for the sum of $270,000. The University was to lease the buildings from Security Trust for one year with the privilege of renewing the lease annually for nineteen additional years. The annual rental was $23,792, and the school had the privilege of buying the property at any time at prices agreed upon in advance. Actually the University was buying back the ground it had sold and the buildings which had been erected thereon with the rent it was paying. This was a means of getting needed rooming space which apparently could not be obtained otherwise; it was probably the only one possible in a state where public education had not been completely accepted as a public responsibility.

The dormitory built in 1922 had never been named and was referred to by its occupants, not critically but somewhat affectionately, as "the shack." Now the board named the three dormitories for former Trustees William O. Bradley, W. C. P. Breckinridge, and W. B. Kinkead.[1] Of all the buildings erected in this period, the President was proudest of the new library, for he considered a library to be the heart of a University. The library, like the dormitories, was erected without any direct appropriation from the legislature. This was done by careful management of the University's funds, the major portion being taken from the school's share of the state inheritance tax. In the spring of 1928 the board authorized the drawing of plans for the first unit of what the President hoped would eventually be a building large enough to house one million volumes. Work was started in 1930, and the building was completed in 1931 at a cost of $430,000. The library was dedicated on October 23, 1931, with Dr. John H. Finley, associate editor of the New York *Times* and former president of New York University, as the principal speaker.

The College of Agriculture gained two badly needed buildings. The Dairy Products Building was erected on the northwest corner of the Experiment Station Farm and faced Rose Street. Containing both classrooms and laboratories, it was opened in 1930. The Agricultural Engineering Building, located just behind the Dairy Building, was authorized by the Board of Trustees in 1930 and completed in 1931.

These ten buildings were not all that the University of

[1] Minutes of Board of Trustees, April 5, 1927, April 11, 17, May 26, September 20, 1928, April 16, 1929; Minutes of Executive Committee, May 18, October 18, 1927, January 27, February 8, March 14, June 14, 23, December 6, 1928, January 17, 1929, June 25, 1930, January 21, 1931; Lexington *Leader*, June 2, 1929; *Kentucky Kernel*, June 22, 1928, January 11, February 1, 8, 9, March 15, May 24, 1929, December 16, 1930.

Kentucky needed; they were simply all that it could afford at the time. McVey constantly kept the school's other housing needs before the board. The biological sciences needed better housing, and they needed if possible to be located in the same building. The Department of Home Economics, located in the basement of the Agriculture Building, needed a building of its own. The College of Engineering needed more laboratory facilities if it were to carry on an adequate research program. Several of the older buildings were served by a central heating plant, but it was not adequate for the greatly expanded campus. By 1928 there were a total of nine separate heating plants in operation. That it would be more economical to have a single plant of sufficient capacity to serve all of the buildings was obvious. The President also mentioned the growing need for a Student Union Building, better quarters for administrative offices and for the College of Commerce, which were located in the two oldest buildings on the campus, a larger armory, and another classroom building similar to McVey Hall. But in the midst of the depression such additions seemed remote, and there were always other problems.

In 1932 the University acquired the use of a building which it had owned for fifty years. James K. Patterson had remained in the house that had been built for the President's Home until his death in 1922. His brother Walter continued to live there until he died ten years later. The Patterson House, as it was usually called, was then converted into a Women's Building and used for meetings of various campus organizations. It served in a very limited way the purposes of a student union building.

With the erection of several new buildings, there was also a change in the names of some of the older ones. The older building which housed the Department of Military Science and the women's gymnasium was renamed

Barker Hall to avoid confusion with the newer Alumni Gymnasium. The Mining Engineering Building was named Norwood Hall in honor of Charles J. Norwood, former dean. The Education Building, which was vacated when the Training School was built, was named Frazee Hall for the former trustee and University business agent, David F. Frazee.[2]

The Graduate School was growing rapidly. In 1930-1931, after excluding duplicates, there were 802 graduate students enrolled, half of these in the summer session. South of the Ohio River there was only one school within five hundred miles of the University of Kentucky which awarded the doctorate. That was Peabody College at Nashville, which limited its degrees to the field of education. The first Ph.D. was awarded by the Graduate School in 1929 to James Anderson Yates for work in education; a year later Russell Smith Park in mathematics received the second doctorate.

In 1931, the University Senate, upon the recommendation of the Graduate School Committee, granted permission to the Department of History to offer work leading toward the Ph.D. The President was not sure that this department was either large enough or strong enough to launch out upon such an ambitious program. In the fall of that year, however, he was able to add to the history staff Dr. Paul H. Clyde, who had been teaching at Ohio State University. At the same time he employed a history teacher who became over the years the department's most productive scholar, Dr. Thomas D. Clark.

The personnel of any university undergoes a gradual

[2] *Kentucky Kernel,* October 23, 27, 1931; Minutes of Board of Trustees, April 17, May 26, 1928, April 16, June 1, September 24, 1929, May 31, September 23, November 5, December 16, 1930, April 14, June 3, December 15, 1931; Minutes of Executive Committtee, October 26, November 16, 1928, July 16, 1929, March 14, 1930, January 21, 1931, May 12, September 18, October 20, 23, 28, 1931, July 16, 1932.

but constant change. Professors retire or accept positions elsewhere. New teachers are hired, either as replacements or because of a growing student body. The year 1928 saw the death of former President Henry S. Barker on April 23. In the succeeding year Emeritus Professor Arthur M. Miller died, and Dr. Glanville Terrell, who had been head of the Department of Philosophy, and Dr. J. W. Pryor, who had headed the Department of Anatomy and Physiology, both retired. This same period during the late twenties and early thirties saw the arrival on the campus of a number of people who remained to make their mark upon the University. James W. Martin came from Emory in 1928 to take over the Bureau of Business Research, and a year later Statie Erikson became head of the Home Economics Department. Coming also at this time were Edward Rannells to head the Art Department and a little later Leo M. Chamberlain in Education, Martin M. White in Psychology, and L. A. Pardue in Physics.

In 1931 it appeared for a time that Dean Taylor would be lost to the University of Pittsburgh, and in 1932 Dean Cooper was asked at what salary he would consider coming to Ohio State. Fortunately for the University of Kentucky, both deans remained, probably at a financial sacrifice in each case.

The need for some type of retirement system at the University had been mentioned by McVey as early as 1921, and at intervals he had brought the matter to the attention of the Board of Trustees or the Executive Committee. The plan which was adopted by the board in December, 1928, was not a pension plan, but a "change of work" plan. When a staff member reached the age of seventy, he would give up his regular position and would be given lighter duties designated by the President. He would receive 20 percent of the average annual salary received during his last five years of active service plus 1 percent of that amount for each year of service in the University. In no case would his compensation be greater than 50 percent of his average annual salary during his last five years of full service. On July 1, 1929, six staff members were given change of work status.[3]

Although a new library building was constructed in 1931, the depression prevented the addition of books as rapidly as had been hoped. In 1928 the University owned 85,797 volumes, and by 1932 the number had grown to 128,587. This number included several gifts, among them 3,000 volumes from Dr. Glanville Terrell, 600 from Dr. Ellen Semple, and 7,000 volumes of government documents from Centre College. The new building made it possible for the University to care adequately for manuscripts and rare books and pamphlets.

A committee was named to solicit gifts for the library. It consisted of two local authors and book collectors, Charles R. Staples and J. Winston Coleman, and two faculty members, Dr. John S. Chambers and Dr. Thomas D. Clark. In particular Dr. Clark did a tremendous amount of collecting for the library, much of it on his own time.

Two museums were established at the University in 1932. The former library building became an anthro-

3 Lexington *Leader*, February 24, 1931; Lexington *Herald*, February 17, 1932; McVey Diary, May 16, 19, 1930, January 10, February 21, May 4, 6, 29, July 15, October 15, 1931, May 12, 1932; Minutes of Board of Trustees, June 13, 1922, September 23, 1924, April 13, May 29, September 28, 1926, May 28, 1927, April 17, September 20, 1928, June 1, September 24, 1929, April 15, May 31, September 23, 1930, June 3, July 1, September 1, December 15, 1931, June 4, 1932; Minutes of Executive Committee, March 16, 1921, May 18, 1928, January 17, March 13, July 1, 16, 1929, May 13, June 10, 1931, September 30, 1932; Minutes of University Senate, May 27, 1927, March 14, December 11, 1928, December 15, 1929, March 16, 1931; *Kentucky Kernel*, February 10, May 4, June 22, 1928, April 12, May 17, June 28, July 5, 1929, September 25, 1931, January 15, February 9, September 20, 1932.

pological and archeological museum, housing the collection gathered by Funkhouser and Webb. The geological museum on the second floor of the Administration Building contained more than ten thousand specimens.

Although the University needed help in the field of public relations, the coming of the depression forced McVey to continue in the role of a one-man public relations bureau for several more years. The number of speeches that he made both in and out of the state would have been impossible for a man with less stamina and must have taxed the energy of one who reached the age of sixty in 1929. In this field Mrs. McVey was of tremendous help. She too made speeches, and she served on the State Illiteracy Commission and on the Lexington Board of Education. The President realized that he gave too much of his time to public relations, but there seemed to be no other way.

He tried to maintain friendly relations with Kentucky's other institutions of higher education both public and private. Usually he succeeded, but at times good relations were affected by matters having little or no connection with the real purposes of education. For example, in 1929 the University of Kentucky decided to drop Centre College from its 1930 football schedule and substitute the University of Virginia, since Virginia belonged to the Southern Conference, of which Kentucky was a member, and Centre did not. As McVey recorded in his diary, "The game has become a grudge game in which hard feelings and even hatred have been aroused." President Turck of Centre favored this step, believing that severing athletic relations would promote greater harmony between the two schools.

Not everyone felt the same way about the matter as did Turck and McVey. In 1931 a group of Kiwanis clubs in central Kentucky petitioned the Board of Trustees of the University to reestablish athletic relations with Centre. In the next year there was a rumor that the legislature was about to call on the University to play Centre in football, and the issue continued to be revived at intervals over a period of several more years.[4]

The University's relations with the state teachers colleges at Richmond, Bowling Green, Morehead, and Murray usually were pleasant, even though they were in a sense in competition for state funds. In 1931 *The Kentucky Kernel* published an editorial which was very critical of the amount of money which had been spent on these colleges, and in addition expressed the opinion that much of this money should have been spent on the University. This brought from the teachers colleges the reaction that might have been expected. When the President of Murray hinted that McVey should not allow such things to appear in a student publication, the President of the University inserted a letter in the *Kernel* indicating his belief that a student newspaper should have freedom of expression, but also made it clear that positions taken by the *Kernel* should not be taken as the official opinions of the administration of the University of Kentucky.

In the winter of 1931-1932 McVey gave much time and thought to the work of a Committee on Education of which he was a member. It had been appointed by the president of the Kentucky Education Association to examine public education in Kentucky from the kinder-

4 *Kentucky Kernel*, March 8, November 1, 27, 1929, April 11, 1930, September 22, December 8, 1931, January 15, 19, March 8, 1932; Thompson, "Books at the University of Kentucky," 65; McVey Diary, January 15, May 10, June 9, October 9, 1930, January 11, June 29, October 27, 29, December 21, 1931, February 17, October 13, 1932; Minutes of Board of Trustees, June 1, 1929, September 22, 1931, June 4, 1932; Minutes of Executive Committee, October 27, 1932; Lexington *Leader*, June 30, 1929, June 24, 1932.

garten through the graduate school and make recommendations to the Kentucky Education Association at its annual convention in April. In December, 1931, James H. Richmond took office as Superintendent of Public Instruction. One of his first proposals was the creation by the legislature of an Educational Commission which would make a more detailed study and report to the legislature in 1934. The legislature took the necessary action, and Governor Ruby Laffoon named McVey as chairman of this commission. This made it necessary for him to coordinate the work of the Educational Commission with that of the K.E.A. committee.

The suggestions of these two groups produced a considerable amount of constructive legislation. A recommended revision and simplification of the state's laws pertaining to education produced a new school code enacted into law in 1934. In the college and university field the chief result was the creation of the Council on Public Higher Education including representatives from the University, the four teachers colleges, and the State Board of Education. This body has done much to promote cooperation and to reduce competition and wasteful duplication of effort. It is unfortunate that the proposal to have the State Superintendent of Public Instruction appointed by a board of nonsalaried laymen instead of being elected was not adopted.

The effect of the depression upon the University was gradual, but it was serious. The total income for 1928-1930 was larger than it had been for the preceding biennium, $5,301,092, of which $3,044,620 came from the state. Agricultural Extension and Home Economics Extension work had been given additional help by the passage of the Capper-Ketcham Act in 1928. This gave to each state $20,000 of federal money per year. An additional $500,000 would be prorated annually among the states on the basis of the ratio of rural population to the total population, the latter gift to be matched by state or local funds.

In 1930 one source of revenue from the state was reduced by a decision of the Supreme Court of the United States. The state had been collecting an inheritance tax upon stock owned in Kentucky corporations regardless of where the deceased owners had lived. The court held that the estates of persons not residents of Kentucky were not subject to the Kentucky inheritance tax. This decision cost the University between $50,000 and $100,000 per year.

In the same year the legislature gave strong consideration to cutting the tax on real property. This would have injured not only education but other state services as well. Fortunately it was not done. On March 22, 1930, McVey wrote in his diary: "The legislature adjourned on Thursday and everybody breathes a sigh of relief." For the 1930-1932 biennium the University received from the state $2,931,639 out of a total income of $5,168,308.

The reduction of income was not so great as might have been expected. Kentucky, being predominantly agricultural, had not yet been affected by the depression to such an extent as had some of the more highly industrialized states. In the summer of 1930, however, a severe drought had its effect. Farm incomes were cut and this was likely to bring a demand for a reduction in taxes.

While the 1932 legislature was wrestling with the question of appropriations for the next biennium, the University was facing the problem of how to meet its obligations for the current year. Receipts from the real estate tax and the inheritance tax had fallen far below expectation. The President, after talking with Judge Richard Stoll, chairman of the Executive Committee, decided that a reduction in all expenditures, including salaries, was the only answer. Effective March 1, 1932, all salaries of $1,300 or less were reduced by 5 percent and those in excess of

$1,300 were reduced by 10 percent. Although this was a serious blow to all employees, it was accepted in a fine spirit. The financial situation, however, grew worse, and within a month it was clear that even this reduced payroll could not be met. The President called a meeting of the University Assembly for March 30. It is not surprising that the attendance was the largest in the history of the organization. The President told them that salaries might have to be cut by as much as 50 percent, but insisted that somehow the University must continue to operate. He appealed for patience and understanding. Several times he was interrupted by applause.

Within a few days two other plans had been devised. McVey had convinced some of the leading businessmen of Lexington that keeping the University open was important to them financially as well as otherwise. They contributed to a fund from which University staff members could borrow at a low rate of interest. Again on April 2 he called the Assembly together and told them that for this month instead of a 50 percent reduction, the University would pay in full all salaries of $100 per month or less and would also pay $100 per month on all salaries that were larger than that amount. In May and June no salaries could be paid.

The University's revenue from the state for the 1932-1934 biennium was more than a million dollars less than it had been for the previous one, $1,786,304 out of a total income of $3,769,427. The total income would have been somewhat smaller had not the Board of Trustees agreed with McVey on the necessity of increasing student fees from $30 to $47 per semester. Those faculty members who taught in the 1932 summer session were paid out of fees collected. In recent years this amount had been supplemented by the state. The plan of paying a maxi-

mum of $100 per month to each person was continued
through the remainder of the 1932 year, but the situation
was helped somewhat by making to those who were paid
on a ten-month basis—and this included most of the
faculty—payments of this amount on July 31 and August
31 when ordinarily they would have received nothing on
these dates.

In 1917 Kentucky's Attorney General, M. M. Logan,
had held that educators were not state officials and hence
were not subject to the state's $5,000 salary limitation. In
1932 the feeling among some taxpayers was so strong that
the question was raised again. At the University only the
salaries of McVey, Dean Cooper, Dean Anderson, and
Dean Melcher were above that figure. The opinion of
Attorney General Bailey P. Wootton coincided with that
of Logan.

Although the University's income dropped during the
depression, its enrollment continued to increase for several
years. In the academic year 1926-1927 there were 2,485
students enrolled in the regular term. In this figure there
were added to the first semester enrollment only those
who had not been enrolled for the first semester; that is to
say, no person was counted twice. In the summer session
of 1927 there were enrolled 1,138, but this number included an unknown number of persons who had attended
during the regular term. In the following year the
registrar began to exclude summer session duplicates, and
so the total figures for any given year became more mean-
ingful. In 1927-1928 the total enrollment was 3,702, in
1928-1929 it was 3,782, in 1929-1930 the figure was 4,241,
in 1930-1931 it was 4,845, and in 1931-1932 it was 4,992.
The College of Arts and Sciences continued to lead all
others in enrollment, having nearly twice as many students
as the College of Engineering, which ranked second. In

December, 1931, McVey told a student convocation that the University of Kentucky ranked third in size in the South, being exceeded only by Tulane University and the University of Texas.

In 1930 a University Personnel Service, long desired by the administration, was established in connection with the Department of Psychology. Dr. James B. Miner, head of that department, was named as director, and Dr. Henry Beaumont, a new assistant professor of psychology who had been employed partly for that purpose, was named as executive secretary.[5]

Two departments in the College of Arts and Sciences were honored during this period. Kentucky's Department of Journalism was placed in Class A by *United States Publisher,* a periodical devoted to newspaper work. In 1930 six paintings by University art students were included in the exhibition of the College Art Association of New York. This was the largest number displayed by any college or university in the country. One of the six, a painting by Norman Neff, took the first prize. In 1931 the University was represented by sixteen etchings and blockprints, and one of these won the first prize in the black-and-white class.

In 1928 the Romany Theater was renamed the Guignol. Under the directorship of Frank Fowler its excellent work

5 Lexington *Leader,* April 14, 1932; Lexington *Herald,* December 17, 1931, April 10, 1932, February 23, 1934; *Kentucky Kernel,* August 7, 1931, September 16, 1932; McVey Diary, January 25, 30, March 22, 1930, September 30, October 1, 2, 21, December 10, 11, 18, 24, 1931, January 23, February 25, 26, 27, 29, March 24, 30, 31, April 1, 2, 3, July 13, September 12, 1932, May 20, December 28, 1933; McVey, *The Gates Open Slowly,* pp. 219-20; Edward Danforth Eddy, Jr., *Colleges For Our Land and Time* (New York, 1957), pp. 178-79; *The University of Kentucky: Its History and Development,* p. 31; Minutes of Board of Trustees, December 17, 1929, April 15, May 31, September 23, 1930, June 4, 1932; Minutes of Executive Committee, November 5, 1930, January 21, 1931; July 13, September 20, 1932.

continued. Receiving especially high praise were the plays "Hay Fever," "Peer Gynt," "Macbeth," "A Doll's House," and "She Stoops to Conquer." The all-student organization known as the Strollers continued to present one production a year.[6]

From time to time humor magazines appear on any college or university campus. At the University of Kentucky this was the day of *The Kampus Kat*. It was published by the journalism fraternity Sigma Delta Chi, and in its early days it won an award for being the best and cleanest college comic paper in the country. By 1932 its quality had dropped considerably, and the President decided that it was time to have a talk with the editor of what he described as this "alleged campus funny paper." He referred to *The Kampus Kat* as being "full of liquor, petting, and suggestive jokes." The editor said that he was printing what the students wanted and that college humor had to be of this type or it would not sell. The President did not ban the magazine from the campus. Instead, he let it continue until it died a natural death.

A Men's Student Council, which had been formed in 1929, felt within a year that it was not being given the share in student government that it should have, and its members threatened to resign. McVey convinced them that such an organization could play an important role in university life, but that a system of complete student government would not be wise. The council accepted this and for the time being continued to play a minor part. By 1932 it found what some of its members considered to be a worthwhile project. It joined in the grow-

6 Lexington *Leader,* June 2, 1929, November 5, 15, 1930, April 23, May 4, 1931; *Kentucky Kernel,* February 17, April 20, September 28, November 2, 1928, September 20, October 11, 1929, September 19, 1930, January 23, March 10, October 6, 16, 20, 27, 1931, October 14, 1932; McVey Diary, March 24, 1930, March 24, December 8, 1931, March 15, 1932.

ing opposition to the head football coach and endeavored to get him fired.[7]

The football team, under the coaching of Harry Gamage, had a poor season in 1927. The next year showed a slight improvement with four wins, three losses, and one tie. In February, 1929, Gamage was given a five-year contract beginning July 1, 1929, and ending July 1, 1934. In the fall of 1929 Kentucky played its first night game, defeating Maryville College by a score of 40 to 0, four of the six touchdowns being made by sophomore halfback John Sims "Shipwreck" Kelly.

The Athletic Association at this time was governed by an Athletic Council consisting of the President of the University, the graduate manager of athletics, three members of the faculty, three alumni, who must reside in Fayette County, and two undergraduates. The members were appointed by the President.

When the 1930 football season opened, Kentucky backers had high hopes. There was even talk of the possibility of an invitation to the Rose Bowl. The first four games were won by large scores. Then came a 19 to 0 defeat at the hands of Alabama, and the season ended with five wins and three losses. The 1931 season was no better; five games were won, two were lost, and two were tied. There was even talk on and off the campus of the need for recruiting players and subsidizing them by giving them some form of employment. The administration would not hear to this. McVey wrote in his diary that too much stress was put upon winning.

Although the 1931 season was disappointing, it did have its exciting moments. "Shipwreck" Kelly's ninety-six

7 McVey Diary, November 7, 25, December 12, 1930, November 11, 1932; *Kentucky Kernel*, February 1, November 15, 1929, March 28, May 23, October 31, 1930, September 22, 25, October 30, 1931, April 8, December 13, 1932; Lexington *Leader*, May 6, 1930; Minutes of Board of Trustees, December 16, 1930.

yard return of an intercepted Washington and Lee pass for one of Kentucky's seven touchdowns in that game was called by a sports statistics bureau the longest run of its kind in the nation that season. Also, a 6 to 6 tie with Tennessee relieved some of the pressure for a new coach and for a renewal of athletic relations with Centre College, which on the same day lost to Chattanooga, 25 to 7.

The 1932 season was even more disappointing. Only four games were won while five were lost. At the close of the season the *Kernel* decided to run a series of editorials on the athletic situation, but the first of these editorials stirred up so much strife on the campus that the editor decided against writing any more. Presently a student petition was presented, asking for the removal of Coach Gamage and the reorganization of the financial management and the personnel of the Athletic Council. The petition carried thirty-eight signatures. Most of the signers were presidents of fraternities, sororities, or other campus organizations.

On the night of December 8 printed but unsigned handbills were scattered over the campus, accusing the coach of exerting undue influence on the selection of football captains over a period of three years. This was denied by members of the football squad, who blamed the agitation upon campus politics. The *Kernel* threatened to conduct an investigation and the Men's Student Council passed a resolution calling for the dismissal of Gamage. In the investigation made by the administration, some changes were made in the membership of the Athletic Council. The head accountant in the Business Office examined the financial condition and practices of the council and declared them sound. Coach Gamage was retained, and student and alumni interest soon turned to other things, such as Kentucky's membership in the newly formed Southeastern Athletic Conference.

Kentucky was becoming known more as a basketball school than a football school. Coached for three years by John Mauer, the basketball team won twelve games and lost six in 1927-1928, won twelve and lost five in 1928-1929, and in 1929-1930 won sixteen and lost only three. In the 1930-1931 season Adolph Rupp began his long tenure as basketball coach for Kentucky. His first team won fifteen games and lost three, and his 1931-1932 team also won fifteen but lost only two. In 1932-1933 Rupp's boys won twenty games, lost three, and were victors in the Southeastern Conference tournament.

Under President McVey's leadership the University had come a long way in fifteen years. Its academic standing was far above what it had been in the Barker period, but there was another honor that he considered essential— membership in the Association of American Universities. This might require further strengthening of the Graduate School, further additions to the physical plant, and a still larger library. The creation of more colleges might help, especially a College of Medicine. All these things McVey had in mind for the decade of the thirties. The depression made their attainment impossible, and it was also tragic that he had to give his attention to athletic squabbles at a time when far more important things were on his mind. Only to his closest friends did he reveal what the depression had done to his dreams for the University of Kentucky. In the words of one of them: "It broke his heart."[8]

8 Minutes of Executive Committee, February 7, 1929; *Kentucky Kernel*, October 11, 1929, November 25, 1931, December 6, 9, 13, 16, 1932; Louisville *Courier-Journal*, December 10, 1932; McVey Diary, October 9, 10, November 26, 1931, November 14, December 3, 4, 6, 7, 21, 27, 1932; Constitution of Athletic Association, Copy of Student Petition, Copy of Anonymous Handbill, Members of Football Squad to McVey, December 5, 10, 1932, McVey to K. C. Babcock, November 9, 1929, McVey Papers; Statement of Dr. John S. Chambers to author.

CHAPTER VIII

HOLDING THE LINE

DURING the middle years of the 1930s the University of Kentucky, like many other institutions, had to be content with maintaining itself without much effort toward growth or expansion. Its policy was to retain the staff as much as possible, even though salaries had to be reduced. When deaths, retirements, or resignations did occur, replacements were often not made. The enrollment dropped at first, but later, as more assistance to students came from the federal government, it climbed to a higher point than it had ever reached. This placed a sore burden on the University, for its income, and chiefly its state support, had declined drastically. Offsetting the stringencies of these times were honors that were received by the University's students and faculty, and a hopeful note was sounded when toward the end of this period the federal government in an attempt to aid the construction industry and the economic situation generally began to make funds available for new buildings.

In December, 1933, President McVey reported to the Board of Trustees that the staff was smaller than it had been for years. During 1933 and 1934 five members of the faculty died, and four retired. Among the deaths was that of Dr. J. Catron Jones, head of the Department of Political Science, who was on leave of absence working for the Federal Power Commission in Washington at the time, while among the retirements were those of J. T. C. Noe from Education and J. Morton Davis from Mathematics, both of whom had served the University for years. Of these nine vacancies, four were heads of departments;

these were filled by the promotion of a member of the department involved. In this way Amry Vandenbosch succeeded Dr. Jones and Ralph N. Maxson became head of the Department of Chemistry. By 1936 occasional additions and replacements were possible. Dr. Cecil C. Carpenter came from Marshall College to take a position as assistant professor of economics, and Dr. Jasper B. Shannon, head of the Department of Political Science at Transylvania College, became assistant professor of political science, replacing Dr. Esther Cole Franklin, who had resigned. The College of Engineering added Frank J. Cheek as professor of sanitary engineering and A. J. Meyer as professor of aeronautical and mechanical engineering.

In 1933 the board had authorized the President of the University to act upon applications which might be received from Jewish professors who wished to leave or were forced to leave Germany. As a result, Dr. Richard Brauer came to the Department of Mathematics as a visiting professor for the year 1933-1934. In 1935 Dr. Fritz John was hired as a regular member of the Department of Mathematics. For the first year his salary was paid half by the Emergency Committee in Aid of Displaced German Scholars and half by the Rockefeller Foundation. The University of Kentucky assumed the committee's share of his salary for his second year and the full amount after that.

Some appointments caused McVey more concern than others because of the nature and importance of the position to be filled. The recommending of teachers and even of department heads could be left largely to the deans— but there were times when deanships became vacant, and two such cases occurred within a two-year period. The President began nearly a year beforehand to think of possible replacements. "A dean of men," he wrote in his diary, "must have patience, courage, a clear mind, and a university outlook." On a later date he wrote that this office of Dean of Men required so much in the way of personality and understanding that it was very difficult to find the qualities. He told the Board of Trustees that the office of dean was one that could make or mar an institution's relationship to the student body.

The problem was finally solved by making two appointments. Dr. T. T. Jones, head of the Department of Ancient Languages, was named as Dean of Men. Lysle W. Croft, who had just received his master's degree in the Department of Psychology was named as assistant dean.

A larger gap was left in the administration by the death of Dean F. Paul Anderson in April, 1934, following an operation. Anderson was nearing the age for change of work at the time of his death, and McVey had already been pondering the question of a suitable replacement. In the meantime, W. E. Freeman served as acting dean.

In March, 1935, the McVeys had as house guests Colonel James H. Graham of Louisville and Mrs. Graham. A 1900 alumnus, Graham had wide experience in the field of engineering. During World War I he had served with the Corps of Engineers of the American Expeditionary Force and had been in charge of the construction of supply depots, docks, and railways. After the armistice he had supervised the repair of over 7,000 miles of highways in France and Germany. Following that duty, he had been named as a member of the United States Liquidation Commission in Europe.

Graham had been awarded the Distinguished Service Medal by the United States government and had been given the rank of Officer in the Legion of Honor by France. His postwar career had included mining and a period in the oil business during which he became president of the Indian Refining Company. In recent years he had served as a consultant in various business and industrial enterprises. Undoubtedly McVey was impressed by this record. He was further impressed by the fact that Graham's knowledge and interests were broader than those of most engineers. He had written a book called *Joseph the Husband of Mary,* which McVey read with some interest. He thought it showed a "wide knowledge of the ancient world" and indicated that the colonel had a "philosophical mind."

While Graham was his guest, McVey asked him if he would be interested in being a dean. Graham replied that he had never thought of it. Ten days later, however, he wrote that he would accept the position if it were offered to him. McVey wrote in his diary that while Graham would give the college some prestige, it was something of an adventure to appoint a man with no academic experience. In May, 1935, the board approved McVey's recommendation of Graham for Dean of the College of Engineering, effective June 1.[1]

Despite the restrictions of the depression, the services of the University to the state were continued, and later some new ones were begun. The Farm and Home Convention was held each January, and growing from it was a successful series of Rural Church Institutes. In 1935 annual training schools were instituted for firemen and police officers; a year later short courses were offered in public health for physicians, nurses, and sanitary inspectors. On an academic level the University could offer the bachelor's

[1] Minutes of Board of Trustees, June 1, September 19, December 14, 1933, May 29, September 20, December 11, 1934, May 30, September 24, 1935; Minutes of Executive Committee, June 23, 1933, January 17, June 30, 1934, January 16, 1935, February 25, July 23, October 14, 1936; McVey Diary, 1933-1935, *passim; Kentucky Kernel,* July 28, 1936; Lexington *Herald,* May 31, June 17, 1935, September 11, 1936.

degree with a major in library science in 1933, and in that same year its four-year course in medical technology was approved by the American Society of Clinical Pathologists.

A novel program to reach the isolated people of eastern Kentucky was begun in 1933 with the establishment of radio-listening centers in that region. Receivers, furnished by various donors, were set up in the mountain area, and people who had never before heard a radio gathered to listen to the University program which was broadcast from 12:45 to 1:30. This work was in charge of Elmer Sulzer, who had given up directing the University band to handle radio and publicity programs. Another facet was added to extension work when Dr. Willem van de Wall came to the University in 1936 at the urging of President McVey to become professor of musical education.[2]

In the spring of 1936 the administration undertook the creation of a Graduate Faculty. The President's letter asking for recommendations brought him the names of everybody who did anything even remotely related to graduate work. Dean Funkhouser reduced the number of names from 135 to 95. While McVey thought this was a rather large Graduate Faculty, he agreed that the list should include all of "the important and really significant people in the various fields."

Meager financial support during the depression years did not, however, halt research and writing. In 1935 the Engineering College began to do research for the State Highway Commission, concentrating upon the testing of materials used in highway construction. In 1934 Kentucky's Experiment Station with the assistance of the Civil Works Administration made a study of assessment, taxation, and sales of farm land in every county in the state. When the project was completed, records of 300,000

2 McVey Diary, 1930-1936, *passim; Kentucky Kernel,* June 26, 1931, January 10, 1933; Lexington *Leader,* August 26, 1934.

transactions were on file and available for further study. The research of Kentucky's agricultural scientists—in particular that of E. S. Good and W. W. Dimock in animal pathology, of W. S. Anderson in genetics, and of W. D. Valleau in plant pathology—was known far beyond the borders of the United States, and requests for their publications came frequently from foreign countries. Other scholars were also active. Eight members of the faculty published books, and well over seventy contributed various articles to the journals. Also during this period President McVey often mentioned to the board or the Executive Committee the advantages of establishing a University Press at Kentucky.[3]

The University of Kentucky and its staff served the federal government during the depression years. The land grant colleges in the seven states which lie partly in the valley of the Tennessee River worked closely with the Tennessee Valley Authority in an effort to solve the economic and social problems of the region. The Association of Land Grant Colleges and Universities appointed a committee to coordinate the help which the association might be able to give to the TVA, and of this committee McVey was chairman. Dean Cooper often advised the TVA in the agricultural field, and W. S. Webb was granted a leave of absence to serve as its supervising archeologist.

In addition to their work with the TVA the staff of the College of Agriculture, the Experiment Station, and Agricultural Extension assisted the federal government with

[3] Lexington *Leader*, April 5, July 17, December 8, 1935, December 1, 1936; *Kentucky Kernel*, December 8, 15, 1933, February 9, 1934, March 19, May 7, 1935, May 12, June 23, 1936; Lexington *Herald*, February 8, April 30, December 18, 1934, January 1, April 8, September 22, 1935; Minutes of Board of Trustees, December 11, 1934, May 30, 1935, April 7, June 4, 1936; Minutes of Executive Committee, January 16, 1935; Minutes of University Senate, November 12, 1934, February 10, April 6, 1936; Louisville *Courier-Journal*, February 6, 1935; *University of Kentucky: Research Publications of Members of the Research Club*, 1935, 1936, and 1937, *passim*; McVey Diary, 1933-1936, *passim*.

the programs of the Agricultural Adjustment Administration, Rural Rehabilitation, and Soil Erosion Control and Land Usage. At the same time the state administration was seeking the full-time service of some of the faculty members. McVey also was active in service during these years. In 1933 he was elected president of the Southern Association of Colleges and Secondary Schools, and in the following year he became president of the Association of Land Grant Colleges and Universities, of which Dean Cooper was secretary-treasurer. Later, in the spring of 1936, McVey was chosen as president of the Kentucky Educational Association. This took an unusual toll of his energy because he had to deliver addresses at all the K.E.A. district conventions, in addition to planning and presiding over the state convention in Louisville.

From time to time honors came to other members of the staff. Paul Clyde was given a leave of absence for the year 1933-1934 to do research in Japan with his expenses paid by the Japanese government. His leave was extended for an additional six months, and he was allowed to work in most of the Japanese mandated islands of the Pacific. J. S. McHargue received the American Society of Agronomy's highest award for his research on the effect of the rarer chemical elements on plants and animals. Twenty-seven members of the faculty were listed in *Who's Who in America for 1934-35.*[4]

Most of the University's public relations continued to

4 McVey Diary, 1933-1936, *passim;* Minutes of Board of Trustees, December 14, 1933, April 5, December 11, 1934, April 16, September 24, December 17, 1935, June 4, September 23, December 8, 1936; Minutes of Executive Committee, March 20, 1933, January 17, 1934, January 16, February 12, October 31, 1935, February 25, April 7, June 16, October 14, 1936; Lexington *Leader,* June 30, 1934; Lexington *Herald,* March 11, 1933, November 22, 1934, April 1, 12, 1936; *Kentucky Kernel,* December 15, 1933, November 9, 23, 1934, February 12, May 17, December 10, 1935, April 21, July 7, 1936; S. J. McCallie to McVey, December 11, 1933, McVey Papers.

rest largely on the President himself. In addition to numerous commencement addresses a year, he made several speeches each week. On occasion he would plan a trip to eastern or western Kentucky with at least twenty speeches scheduled in advance. He did not make a direct attempt to publicize the University in these talks, but they were no doubt beneficial to the institution. Mrs. McVey and Dean Sarah Blanding also did a considerable amount of public relations work, speaking to high school groups and to women's clubs in many parts of the state. At times the President suggested to the board the creation of a Division of Public Relations which would include "alumni relations, publicity, extension and a placement bureau." But financial conditions prevented this suggestion being realized, and the President continued to carry a large part of the load.

The McVeys did not encourage people to come to the University and then ignore them. The President's office door was always open to students, his busy schedule notwithstanding. Every Wednesday afternoon there was a tea for students at Maxwell Place. At commencement time the President always provided at his own expense a senior breakfast on his lawn. By 1936 nearly six hundred persons attended this breakfast.

The effect of the depression was much in evidence when registration for the second semester of the year 1932-1933 was held. Requests for delay in payment of fees were more numerous than ever before. Some students would not have been in school at all had it not been for help provided by the federal government. By January, 1934, funds from the Civil Works Administration were financing work on campus projects for 106 students. In December the President reported that 279 students were receiving federal assistance. The early years of the Roosevelt administration saw a slight decrease in the amount of federal money available for work in the field of agriculture. In 1935, however, the loss was more than restored by passage of the Bankhead-Jones Act, which provided $1,000,000 a year for agricultural research, to be increased by an equal amount until a maximum of $5,000,000 was reached, to be divided in accordance with the ratio of rural population in any state to total rural population.

The decrease in revenue received from the state in the 1932-1934 biennium forced the University to cut all salaries 10 percent and to raise fees from $30 to $47 a semester. This put the University at a disadvantage in the effort to attract students, because the state teachers colleges were charging only $10 a semester.

Money was still owed to the faculty on salaries which had not been paid in full in the first half of 1932. In August, 1934, one-half of the remaining amount owed on 1931-1932 salaries was paid. The balance then left unpaid was only 7 percent of the back salary owed to the faculty as of June 30, 1932.[5]

Prior to 1934 the state had been giving to the University one-half of the amount collected in the form of inheritance taxes and 6.7 percent of the amount raised by the tax on real property. The legislature of that year, as a part of a broad reorganization bill, repealed the laws providing for this method of distribution and put the institution on an appropriation basis. The only question was how the money for this and the state's other obligations was to be raised. The Laffoon administration favored a retail sales tax. The legislature had been called into special session in August, 1933, and a sales tax bill was defeated in the House. When the regular session met in January, 1934, it passed some excellent laws, but no revenue bill, and so a

[5] McVey Diary, 1933-1936, *passim;* Minutes of Board of Trustees, April 19, 1933, September 20, December 11, 1934, April 16, September 24, 1935, April 7, 1936; Minutes of Executive Committee, June 16, 1936; Lexington *Herald,* February 11, 1934, October 4, 1936; Louisville *Courier-Journal,* June 14, 1936; *Kentucky Kernel,* May 18, September 14, 1934; Lexington *Leader,* November 17, 1935; Eddy, *Colleges for Our Land and Time,* 169.

special session was called to meet on May 9. In June it enacted a 3 percent sales tax by a narrow margin. An income tax passed by the House failed to pass the Senate.

The state's appropriation to the University for 1934-1936 was greater than for the preceding biennium, but it was still far below what it had been in predepression days. The school's revenue from that source was $2,071,820, and its total income from all sources was $4,660,598.

The sales tax became an issue in the 1935 gubernatorial campaign. A. B. Chandler, who as lieutenant governor had been a vigorous opponent of this type of tax, won the governorship. The sales tax was repealed, and an income tax was put in its place. The University's total income for the 1936-1938 biennium was $5,226,303, and of this amount $1,874,072 was appropriated by the state.

The effect of the depression upon enrollment was seen in a drop to a low of 3,822 during 1933-1934, but two years later, enrollment reached a new high of 5,195. A visitor to the campus in 1936 would have found only the buildings which were there in 1932. The increased enrollment was being crowded into the same amount of space as was used four years earlier.

Improvements which were completed during this period were accomplished largely through the use of federal funds. Streets adjoining the campus—Limestone, Euclid, and Rose—were widened, and campus walks and drives were improved. In 1934 a statue of James K. Patterson, executed by Augustus Lukeman, was unveiled behind the Administration Building. Both Patterson and his brother Walter had left money to be used for this purpose.[6]

[6] Minutes of Board of Trustees, June 1, August 14, 15, 19, September 1, 19, 1933, April 5, May 29, September 20, 30, 1934, May 30, September 24, 1935, September 21, 1936; Minutes of Executive Committee, February 21, July 17, 1934, March 13, 1935, March 9, 1936; McVey Diary, 1933-1936, *passim; The University of Kentucky: Its History and Development,* p. 31; Lexington *Leader,* March 30, 1934.

An important part of the legislation passed in 1934 was that which created the Council on Public Higher Education. This body consisted of the Governor, the Superintendent of Public Instruction, the Presidents of the University and of each of the four teachers colleges, the Dean of the University's College of Education, three members of the Board of Trustees of the University, one member of the Board of Regents of each teachers college, and two lay members. The council did very effective work in coordinating curricula, fees, and lengths of summer sessions. Each of the five institutions was required to submit its budget to the council, which might make some adjustments before submitting them to the State Budget Commission.

In 1936 the Council on Public Higher Education took a significant step in coordinating the work in professional education at the five schools. After preliminary work by the five presidents, the council voted to eliminate all graduate work at the four colleges, which offered it only in the field of education, and to concentrate this at the University. In return the University would not offer freshman or sophomore work in education. Its College of Education would thus become a professional school requiring two years of college work for entrance. A student who came to the University expecting to major in education would now do his first two years of work in the College of Arts and Sciences. The council also required the four colleges to raise their fees from $10 to $25 per semester.

It was in 1936, too, that the University Senate added to the requirements for a Master's degree a reading knowledge of a foreign language and an average of *B* instead of *C* in all work done. To strengthen their undergraduate programs, several departments required their majors to pass comprehensive examinations in the senior year. In 1933 this plan was adopted by the Departments of Anatomy, Philosophy, Physics, and Zoology. In 1936 the same requirement had been added in Economics, German, Journalism, Physical Education, Political Science, Romance Languages, and Sociology.

It was a source of pride to the University when, in 1933, one of its graduates, Thomas Hunt Morgan, was awarded the Nobel prize for his research in the field of medicine. Morgan, a member of the class of 1886, had earned his M.S. and Ph.D. degrees from Johns Hopkins. He had been given honorary degrees by McGill, California, Edinburgh, Michigan, and Kentucky.

In competition for Rhodes scholarships, Kentucky had been grouped with North Central states, and the competition had usually been too much for the state of Kentucky with its low-ranking public school system. The President of the University was, therefore, especially pleased when, in 1935, a University of Kentucky senior, Elvis Stahr, was a successful candidate. Stahr graduated from the University of Kentucky in the following June with a perfect standing.[7]

The period from 1932 to 1936 saw the continuation of most of the traditional student activities and the addition of a few new ones. In April, 1936, a group of students came to see the President about the possibility of holding an antiwar meeting on the campus. College students all over the country were troubled by the world situation, and meetings of this kind had been held on several campuses. "In some colleges," said McVey in his diary, "the authorities denied the students the right of assembly,

7 Lexington *Leader*, December 2, 1935; Minutes of Board of Trustees, May 30, December 17, 1935, April 7, June 4, 1936; Minutes of Executive Committee, October 31, 1935; McVey Diary, 1933-1936, *passim;* Minutes of University Senate, April 17, 1933, March 9, 1936; *Kentucky Kernel,* February 7, October 24, December 12, 1933, January 8, March 2, April 10, November 27, December 11, 1934, February 12, March 19, October 15, November 19, December 3, 1935, February 7, 18, March 20, May 5, 19, September 18, December 8, 1936.

but here I gave them all liberty except I refused the request for a parade. The students did not press this point, so there was no difficulty about it." When the meeting was held on April 22, the principal speakers were a faculty member, a student, and a clergyman. According to the *Kernel,* the result was "an orderly, well-presented, thoughtful discussion of the problems which are challenging the attention of the general public and students."

Not all student activities were so well conducted as this one. Earlier in the same school year the Men's Student Council had declared the elections for class officers void because there was evidence that ballot boxes had been stuffed. The Student Council which took this vigorous action was constituted differently from its predecessor. The earlier council had been elected by the students, and in the selection of its members there was the same intense rivalry that existed in the election of class officers. At the beginning of the 1933-1934 school year, McVey had provided for a new type of student council, with all its members either appointed or ex officio. According to the *Kernel,* this change was made "to avoid unfair political activity and unfair elections." The *Kernel* may have been right about the long-range reason. A more immediate reason may have been the efforts of the old Student Council to get rid of football coach Harry Gamage, whose contract had still a year to run.

Coach Gamage's 1933 football season was little better than the preceding one, Kentucky winning five games and losing five. Before the last game was played, he tendered his resignation effective June 30, 1934. The search for a new coach started immediately, and it may have begun before Gamage's resignation. At its meeting in December, 1933, the Board of Trustees approved the appointment of C. A. (Chet) Wynne as Gamage's successor, with a three-year contract. Wynne had been quite successful as head football coach at the Alabama Polytechnic Institute, and great things were expected of him. Soon after his arrival in Lexington, Wynne made a brief talk at a Board of Commerce meeting. McVey was impressed by Wynne's having earned a law degree. He was pleased, too, when the coach, speaking at a church dinner, quoted from Shelley and Sir Walter Scott. "In this," McVey wrote, "he did something that no football coach has done before . . . so far as I know."

In March, 1934, Wynne accepted the additional duties of Director of Athletics, with S. A. Boles, who remained as graduate manager, responsible for ticket sales. This unification was needed, but it may have been a mistake to favor one coach over the others.

The football record under Wynne was not much improved over that of Gamage. Basketball offered, however, a succession of winning seasons, with one conference championship and one co-championship. Of the students' reactions to athletics, McVey wrote in his diary: "Our student body is a nice one, but it is still adolescent."[8]

8 *Kentucky Kernel,* February 3, September 26, October 6, November 24, 1933, March 9, 27, 1934, October 15, November 22, 1935, April 24, November 17, 24, 1936; Minutes of Board of Trustees, December 14, 1933, April 6, 1937; McVey Diary, 1933-1936, *passim;* Lexington *Herald,* December 18, 1934.

CHAPTER IX

BRICKS AND MORTAR

IT WAS the federal government's effort to stimulate the construction industry and to put men back to work that made possible the erection of a new group of buildings on the campus. In May, 1933, Omicron Delta Kappa initiated a fund drive for a Student Union Building. Each fraternity was asked to give one dollar for each initiate. *The Kentucky Kernel* pledged $500 for the first year and $1,000 each year thereafter for twenty years. In January, 1934, an ODK committee came before the Executive Committee of the Board of Trustees and offered to ask each student in the University to give four dollars a year toward the support of such a project. In a period when some students were spending as little as thirty-five cents a day for food, raising money in this way was going to be difficult. The Executive Committee was sympathetic, however, and authorized McVey to investigate the possibility of obtaining a loan for this purpose from the Public Works Administration. Correspondence with this agency brought no immediate results. There was the possibility of a 45 percent grant and a 55 percent loan, but the board in the spring of 1935 was not sure that the building would produce sufficient revenue to repay the loan.

Nevertheless, it was decided that application should be made for funds to erect a Student Union and other needed buildings. Shortly after Colonel James H. Graham became Dean of the College of Engineering, he was named the liaison officer to carry on negotiations with the government. By the end of 1935 there were plans for a Student

Union Building, three Engineering annexes, an Experiment Station annex, a Tobacco Research Laboratory, a Law Building, and a central heating plant. About half of the cost would be covered by a PWA grant. The remainder would be raised by the sale of bonds, a procedure which received the sanction of the Kentucky Court of Appeals.

An architect would prepare plans for the Student Union Building, but Dean Graham and other members of the staff of the College of Engineering would supervise the construction. While plans were being drawn, the *Kernel* in an editorial complained that student groups were not being consulted, that a swimming pool, which students had hoped for, was being omitted, and that the ballroom was not to be as large as had been expected. Further objection was raised to the plan of devoting the basement floor to business enterprises such as a barbershop, a cafeteria, and a grill. McVey replied to the editor that suggestions from students would be welcomed and given every consideration, but that the University could not build the Waldorf-Astoria or the Michigan Union with the amount available for the building and that interest and payments on the building must be met every year for the next twenty-five years.

Ground was broken on April 6, 1936, in ceremonies conducted by ODK, which had initiated the idea for the building four years earlier, and the building was completed in 1938. The Student Union had lounges, offices, a music room, and game rooms on its main floor. The top floor included a ballroom, two small meeting rooms, and a mezzanine. The cafeteria and grill were in the basement and were operated by a private company until the end of 1940, when by mutual agreement this function was taken over by the University.

New space for the College of Engineering was added in

three stages: a two-story south wing extending eastward from the rear of Mechanical Hall, a northward extension of a one-story shop section and the addition of a second story to it, and a two-story west wing. This required the razing of the old mechanical and electrical engineering laboratories built in the 1890s. This new construction made it possible to concentrate all engineering activities under one roof.

The Experiment Station annex was made necessary by the added personnel and increased amount of work resulting from the agricultural legislation of the Roosevelt administration. It gave the Station additional office space, larger quarters in which to prepare bulletins for mailing, and room for the expansion of its library.

The new Law Building was located northwest of the library. Like the Student Union and the Engineering Quadrangle, its architecture was functional. In addition to classrooms, offices, and a large library, there was a courtroom, complete in every detail. It was named Lafferty Hall in honor of the founder and first Dean of the College of Law.

Some planning for a central heating plant had been done by the College of Engineering before the money for the plant was available. When Graham became dean, the plans were pushed to completion and were ready when PWA funds were obtained. Several contracts were let, since the project involved not only a building, but massive equipment and the laying of steam pipes to the various buildings on the campus.[1]

[1] McVey Diary, 1933-1937, *passim; Kentucky Kernel,* May 12, 1933, March 31, April 2, 1936, February 23, 1937; Lexington *Herald,* July 25, 1937; Minutes of Board of Trustees, June 1, 1933, September 20, 1934, May 30, September 24, November 15, 18, December 7, 1935, January 14, 1936, April 6, 1937, April 5, June 3, 1938, September 17, 1940; Minutes of Executive Committee, January 17, February 21, October 23, 1934, February 12, June 27, July 18, 1935, February 25, May 5, 22, June 16, July 23, 1936, December 14, 1937, October 28, November 22, 1940, January 18, 1941.

While these buildings were being constructed, a second PWA grant and the sale of additional bonds made possible the planning of three more buildings. This group consisted of a third dormitory for women, a building for the biological sciences, and a Home Economics Building. The new dormitory for women was attached to Boyd Hall and paralleled Euclid Avenue. While under construction it was referred to as a wing of the older building. Later it was named Jewell Hall in honor of Mrs. McVey, formerly Dean of Women Frances Jewell.

For a building to house the Department of Home Economics, several locations were considered. The site finally selected placed the building southeast of Memorial Hall. When this three-story structure was completed in 1940, Home Economics was finally able to move out of the basement of the Agricultural Building. The building later was named in honor of Dr. Statie Erikson, who for many years was head of the department.

The Biological Science Building, which was built in two stages, was started in 1937 and finished in 1940. The major portion of the building contained three floors, a basement, and a subbasement. With a central tower rising to a height of six stories and bearing the seal of the University of Kentucky near the top, it is still one of the most impressive structures on the campus. It provided space for the Departments of Anatomy and Physiology, Bacteriology, and Zoology. Rooms not needed by these departments at the time were assigned to the Department of Art.

The ROTC regiment at the University was rapidly outgrowing Buell Armory, and there was a plan to enlarge the building by using materials salvaged from the old engineering building and employing WPA labor. After many discouraging delays, the project was completed in 1939. The drill floor was extended eastward, and an ell was added to the extended portion. In this way the size of the floor was more than doubled. A basement under the new portion provided adequate space for a rifle range.[2]

In June, 1940, Dean Graham reported that the Viking Foundation, through one of its officials, the Swedish industrialist Axel Wenner-Gren, had indicated that it might be willing to build and equip an aeronautical research laboratory on the Kentucky campus. If this were done, the Mawen Motor Corporation, in which Wenner-Gren was the chief stockholder, would expect to use the laboratory for testing purposes. This corporation for the past three years had employed Professor A. J. Meyer of the College of Engineering as a consultant in its effort to develop an improved type of internal combustion engine.

At the next meeting of the Executive Committee, Graham appeared with a definite offer from the Viking Foundation and also with authority to act as its agent. The foundation would erect a building at a cost not to exceed $30,000 and would donate it to the University. The cost of the equipment and its installation was not to exceed $50,000. This, too, would be donated to the University. The Mawen Motor Corporation in return for the use of the laboratory would pay for its operation and upkeep. The Executive Committee accepted this offer with the understanding that two rooms in the building might be used by the College of Engineering, that courses might be offered in the building provided they did not interfere with its use by the corporation, and that some engineering students might, with the approval of Dean Graham, be employed in the laboratory.

[2] Minutes of Executive Committee, November 7, 1936, July 6, September 21, November 24, December 14, 1937, February 23, August 27, November 3, 1938, March 15, 1939, February 8, 1940; Minutes of Board of Trustees, June 3, December 14, 1937, August 3, September 20, 1938, April 4, June 2, September 19, 1939, September 17, 1940; McVey Diary, 1936-1940, *passim;* Lexington *Herald-Leader,* March 26, 1939.

The amount needed to erect and equip the building had been badly underestimated. Instead of $80,000 it was found that $150,000 would be necessary. The additional $70,000 was provided by the Viking Foundation, and the laboratory went into operation early in 1941. The erection of many new buildings on the campus left vacant several older buildings into which overcrowded departments could expand. The Physics Department retained its half of the Civil Engineering and Physics Building and expanded into the other half, which had been occupied by Civil Engineering. The Botany Department was moved from White Hall to Norwood Hall, which had been vacated by Mining Engineering. This left all of White Hall to the badly overcrowded College of Commerce. The old law building was given to the Department of Hygiene and Public Health, and the Department of Psychology thus gained all of Neville Hall. The radio broadcasting studios were given the top floor of McVey Hall where the University Commons had been. The removal of Bacteriology from the basement of Kastle Hall left all of that building for the Department of Chemistry.

McVey realized that this building program did not meet all the needs of the University, and he brought this to the attention of the board at every opportunity. More dormitories were needed both for men and for women. The Administration Building, the oldest building on the campus, would eventually have to be replaced. An adequate Fine Arts Building where music, art, and dramatics could be brought together under one roof should not be long postponed. A large museum building where the various collections could be brought together was suggested. The College of Agriculture needed several buildings, the most urgent being new barns for the dairy department.

The President admitted the need for a larger gymnasium, but there were others who gave such a building a higher priority than did he. Students, alumni, state officials, city officials, and the more sports-minded Kentuckians were talking of the need for a fieldhouse. In October, 1939, the *Kernel* admitted that plans for the fieldhouse were practically at a standstill until a definite site had been chosen. An attempt to purchase the property across Euclid Avenue from Stoll Field failed because the price was too high. War had started in Europe, and the fieldhouse idea was forced into the background. The types of buildings just erected or still being erected were more essential to the real purposes of education.[3]

The construction program of the last years of the McVey administration was not accomplished without controversy. McVey remarked that there would be criticism and dissatisfaction because the new structures had discarded the cornice and old adornments that added to expense in building. Prophetically he suggested that some would criticize certain buildings because they did not look like courthouses. He defended them for one reason if for no other, namely, that there was more building for less money. Upon another occasion he defended the new style by the remark that in an age of steel and concrete it was necessary to modify the style of a structure to conform to the materials.

As the building program progressed, criticisms of a more serious nature were voiced. Because of the expectation that the new buildings would eventually be air-conditioned, they were not equipped with windows that

[3] Minutes of Executive Committee, October 14, November 7, 1936, June 28, July 12, November 22, 1940, January 17, 1941; Minutes of Board of Trustees, June 3, 1937, September 20, December 13, 1938, April 4, September 19, 1939, September 17, 1940; McVey Diary, April 5, 19, 1939, June 28, 1940, March 2, 1941; *Kentucky Kernel*, October 9, December 1, 1936, March 24, April 4, 7, October 6, 1939.

could be opened. In the case of the Student Union Building it was expected that in the meantime the problem of ventilation could be solved with a system of fans, but this did not prove satisfactory. Since it was not likely that money for air-conditioning would be available in the near future, other windows had to be installed.

The roofs of three of the new buildings developed leaks. Although these were repaired at comparatively little cost, they provided additional grounds of criticism. Much of the criticism was directed toward Dean Graham, who had supervised the construction of new buildings. He was also serving as a consultant for a construction program being carried on by the state, the main units of which were an office building, a prison, and a mental hospital. It was his feeling that some of the agitation was started by persons who were disappointed at not getting contracts for construction, wiring, plumbing, or architectural work, and McVey was inclined to agree with him. Also mixed with the criticism was a controversy between Graham and one of the professors of engineering. This disagreement originated over the design and construction of the heating plant and was only settled, more or less, in the spring of 1940.

Of the building program McVey wrote in his diary: "It is rather discouraging, too, that no one comes to help, or any alumnus writes to the papers supporting the building program."[4]

[4] *Kentucky Kernel*, January 17, 20, 1939, January 23, May 3, 7, 8, 10, 14, 17, 1940, May 30, 1941; McVey Diary, 1936-1940, *passim;* Minutes of Board of Trustees, December 23, 1936, April 4, June 2, September 19, December 15, 1939, April 2, June 7, September 17, 1940; Minutes of Executive Committee, July 23, 1936, December 14, 1937, March 22, 1938.

CHAPTER X

MORE CHANGES

THE PERIOD between 1937 and 1941 was a time of survey-
ing the administration, of assessing directions before the
change that lay just ahead with President McVey's ap-
proaching retirement, as well as a time of physical expansion of the University. In the spring of 1937 McVey
invited Raymond M. Hughes, President Emeritus of Iowa
State College, to make a survey of the University of Kentucky and submit his recommendations. Hughes was
experienced in this kind of work, for it had become a
hobby with him since his retirement.

In his report Hughes said of Graham: "The Dean is
moving toward a new plan of engineering education that
seems wholly good. He ought to have all possible support
in trying out his plan." On the critical side, however, he
remarked that Engineering had 418 students and a budget
of $115,000 while the College of Commerce was teaching
833 students with a $40,000 budget. Hughes admitted
that Engineering was always expensive, but he thought
that from $5,000 to $10,000 could be shifted from the
Engineering budget to the Commerce budget for the
coming year.

The Hughes report was especially critical of the number
of small classes at the University. During the spring
semester, 1935-1936, 190 classes, or 20.5 percent of those
offered, had five students or less, and 127 or 13.7 percent
of those scheduled had between six and ten students.
Hughes thought that this indicated either needless expense
from having too many instructors or overworked instructors. It was his belief that lower division classes should

not be taught with less than sixteen members and upper division classes with less than twelve. With the exception of independent research, Hughes felt that graduate courses should not be given to less than eight persons. In his next report to the Board of Trustees, McVey expressed the opinion that the problem was not so serious as Hughes seemed to think, but, nevertheless, it was a problem. He had appointed a committee of professors to look into the matter. The President's own suggestions were limitations upon numbers, staggering of courses every other year, and spreading the enrollment over the whole day so as to lessen the strain upon the popular second, third, and fourth hours.

Early in 1936 McVey had appointed a Committee on the State of the University. It consisted of twenty-eight of the younger members of the staff with Neil Plummer, of the Journalism Department, as chairman. After numerous meetings, the committee submitted a very long report in July, 1937, which pointed out a number of weaknesses among the faculty. Among them was the responsibility of faculty members for keeping abreast of current research. Staff use of the general library, the committee found, was shockingly small. Figures from the circulation department of the library showed that only 125 staff members, out of a total of more than 400, borrowed one or more books in the fiscal year 1935-1936. Another failing the committee pointed out was the abuse of the teaching position in criticizing other departments or faculty members or the departmental situation. Faculty members should also use tact in the presentation of subject matter and should feel a responsibility for promoting a friendly feeling for the University among the citizens of the state. Another complaint received by the chairman of this committee was that too many departments left too much of their lower division teaching to instructors and graduate assistants.

How much good, if any, had been accomplished by all of this work it is impossible to say. Perhaps if nothing more, it stimulated some thinking which would bear fruit later on. The Senate discussed the report at great length, but, as McVey recorded in his diary, that body "was not keen about any of it."[1]

The President at times became discouraged about the difficulty encountered in trying to accomplish anything in the Senate. This group, which included all staff members having the rank of assistant professor or higher, was becoming unwieldly, though McVey felt that this was "the democratic way and so must be adhered to." But later entries in his diary show that he was coming to think that too much power rested in the Senate. Then in the last meeting before his retirement he wrote: "I thought I would say some things about the need of reorganization of the Senate, but concluded that I might be misunderstood."

A sign of the growing maturity of the University of Kentucky was the increase in publications from the faculty. The four years from 1937 to 1941 saw the publication of ten books by faculty members, with the Department of History the most productive of any one department. Numerous articles were also published by various members of the staff; the sciences were especially productive in this area. At the time of a survey in 1938 Dean Funkhouser led all others with a total of 112 articles.

McVey recognized the importance of research and publication and attempted to find ways in which the University might aid scholars to have the results of their work

[1] Minutes of Board of Trustees, April 6, 1937, June 2, 1939; Minutes of University Senate, November 8, 1937, January 10, February 14, 1938; McVey Diary, November 8, 1937, January 10, 1938; R. M. Hughes, "Partial Survey of University of Kentucky," 23 pp. typescript, University of Kentucky Archives; "Report of Committee on the State of the University," General File, University of Kentucky Archives.

made available. Commercial presses had to consider profits, and scholarly works even though their contribution to the world's store of knowledge might be great could not always be depended upon to pay the cost of publishing. The creation of a University Press would have been the answer, but money for such a project was not available. McVey thought that a beginning might be made by utilizing profits made by the Kernel Press. A portion of the Margaret Voorhies Haggin Trust, which had been created in 1938 by Mrs. Haggin in memory of her late husband James Ben Ali Haggin, former owner of Elmendorf Farm near Lexington, was used to finance scholarly publications. A committee on publications was created to consider manuscripts submitted to it. Several books were partially financed by these funds, some being published by commercial presses and others by the Princeton University Press.

In addition to the research carried on by individuals, there were always cooperative projects in progress. One of these was the Bureau of School Service's project for improving the diet of rural Kentuckians by introducing teaching materials pertaining to the cultivation of vegetables, the raising of poultry, and the reclaiming of worn-out land into the curricula of the first four grades, a long-term project begun in 1939 with the backing of the Alfred P. Sloan Foundation. In two counties which lay in the foothills of the Kentucky mountains, four experimental and four control schools were selected. It was hoped that some of the lessons learned by the children in the experimental schools would be carried home to their parents.

One need of the University occasionally brought before the board by McVey was for a museum building to house the various collections of the University. The Geology Department had an extensive collection, part of it located in Miller Hall and part on the second floor of the Administration Building. The Botany Department had about 25,000 specimens in its quarters in what had been the Mining Engineering Building. The work of Professor Webb with WPA help had filled the Museum of Archeology and Anthropology, and many specimens were stored in the service building of the Department of Buildings and Grounds. None of these buildings had adequate display facilities, and none was fireproof.

The University library increased in size from 212,738 volumes in 1937 to 302,889 in 1941. This made it fifth largest among libraries in the southern states. It was improving in quality as well. It was acquiring valuable source materials on Kentucky and the Ohio Valley, including rare books, manuscripts, and newspapers. So many state documents were moved from Frankfort to Lexington that the basement of Memorial Hall had to be fitted with stacks so that it could serve as a library annex. McVey took part in discussions held by thirteen midwestern universities to consider the possibility of a central storage building in the Chicago area for books and materials that were used rarely and recommended the plan to the Board of Trustees.[2]

That the growth of the University, together with other public services which seemed demanded by the increasing complexity of twentieth-century America, could be hampered by the somewhat conservative fiscal attitude in Kentucky was suggested in a 1940 ruling of the Kentucky

2 McVey Diary, 1937-1940, *passim; University of Kentucky: Research Publications of Members of the Research Club*, 1937-1941, *passim;* Thompson, "Books at the University of Kentucky," p. 65; Minutes of Board of Trustees, September 19, 1939, June 7, December 10, 1940, June 5, 1941; Minutes of Executive Committee, February 24, November 24, 1937, July 28, 1938, April 22, 1941; *Kentucky Kernel,* June 14, October 26, 1937, March 17, 1939, October 4, 1940, March 11, 1941; Louisville *Courier-Journal,* December 3, 1939; Lexington *Herald,* May 28, 1940.

Court of Appeals. In an apparent revision of earlier rulings the court held that the head librarian of the Louisville Free Public Library was a public officer and was therefore subject to the state's constitutional salary limit of $5,000 a year. Under this latest ruling, some fifteen persons at the University would be immediately affected, but more serious for the future would be the possible depressing of all salaries at the institution and the difficulties this would create in recruiting new members of the faculty. The state's Attorney General, however, ruled that income from the Haggin Trust could be used to supplement faculty salaries, if necessary.

The plans for the development of the University were disturbed when the agreement between the University and the teachers colleges was canceled. In 1940 the Council on Public Higher Education, reversing its stand four years earlier, permitted the teachers colleges once again to offer graduate work in education. The University then returned to its former practice of admitting students to the College of Education before they had reached their junior year.

Enrollment during these years showed a rather steady increase, rising to a peak of 6,242 in 1940-1941, which was not exceeded until after World War II.[3]

Since 1933 the Student Council had consisted entirely of appointed and ex officio members. By 1939 the students wanted a student legislature with all members elected by the student body. A constitution drawn up by a student-faculty committee was approved by the University Senate

[3] Lexington *Herald,* May 28, October 10, 1940; *Kentucky Kernel,* September 20, 1940; *The University of Kentucky: Its History and Development,* pp. 22, 31; McVey Diary, 1937-1940, *passim;* Minutes of Board of Trustees, February 16, 23, 26, April 6, June 3, 1937, April 5, 1938, March 7, 21, April 25, June 2, December 8, 1939, February 27, June 7, September 17, 1940, March 18, 28, April 25, 1941; Minutes of Executive Committee, December 14, 1937, June 18, 1939.

and ratified by a large majority of the sophomore, junior, and senior classes. It provided for a Student Government Association of twenty-five members elected by the student body. The principal officers were to be a president, a men's vice president, and a women's vice president. The other twenty-two members were to constitute a Student Legislature. The freshman class might elect two of these. The other twenty members were to be chosen by upper-classmen and would represent colleges rather than classes. Representation would be in accordance with the ratio that the enrollment of any college bore to the enrollment of the University. In October, 1939, elections were held under the supervision of a faculty-student committee, and the system went into effect at once. Faculty-student co-operation was achieved by having the legislature do most of its work in committees most of which contained faculty members either appointed by the President or ex officio.

The 1937 football season of the University was highly unsatisfactory to fans. Early in 1938 Coach Wynne tendered his resignation, and a reorganization was put into effect. It was planned to bring athletics more fully under the control of the University. A Department of Athletics was created in the College of Arts and Sciences. Coaches were to be faculty members in this department, and they like any other faculty members would be recommended to the President and to the Board of Trustees by their superiors. Bernie Shively, who during the Wynne period had been in the Department of Physical Education, was named as Director of Athletics. A. D. Kirwan, a former football star and 1926 graduate of the University was named as head football coach. He had been quite success-ful as a coach at Louisville's DuPont Manual High School. There would be an Advisory Council on Athletics ap-pointed by the President. He and the president of the

Alumni Association would be ex officio members. From the faculty he would appoint a vice chairman and three other members. The other appointees would be two students. Faculty members would be appointed for three-year periods and students for two years.

The new organization did not produce any championship football teams, but criticism from the fans was reduced to a minimum. When the 1938 season ended with seven losses and only two victories, McVey remarked in his diary: "It is rather remarkable in view of the many lost games of this season that the enthusiasm should keep up. I think this is due to the new set-up, the character of the men leading the program, and the hope for the future."[4]

At the meeting of the Board of Trustees on June 2, 1939, McVey reminded the members that on November 10 he would reach the compulsory retirement age of seventy. The board immediately passed a motion extending his term to July 1, 1940, and asking that the chairman appoint a committee to recommend a successor. The chairman appointed two committees. From the board he appointed four trustees, with Judge Stoll as chairman. From the faculty he named an advisory committee of four, two of whom were deans. Some faculty members were not pleased when they learned that the faculty committee was only advisory and that the faculty members had been appointed by the Governor instead of by the University Senate. There followed much discussion, but no change.

McVey had not expected to play any role in the choice of his successor beyond that of advising on the question of qualifications which should be sought. Nevertheless, he

---

[4] *Kentucky Kernel*, October 20, 21, 26, 1937, January 14, 21, February 15, 1938, May 16, September 22, 26, October 3, 24, 31, 1939; McVey Diary, 1937-1939, *passim*; Minutes of University Senate, May 31, 1939; Minutes of Executive Committee, October 20, 1937; Minutes of Board of Trustees, June 2, 1939.

was asked by committee members to make recommendations. On more than one occasion he did so, after corresponding with many university presidents and heads of educational foundations. Some of these he visited personally. Members of the committee did some of the preliminary work, and finally a list of about seventy-five names was compiled. On June 7, 1940, on the committee's recommendation, the Board of Trustees named Dean Cooper as acting President effective July 1, 1940, and gave to McVey change-of-work status as professor of agricultural economics.

As retirement approached, the McVeys were honored in many ways. At the University's first outdoor commencement in June, 1938, Mrs. McVey had been given the Algernon Sidney Sullivan Medallion, the highest award that the University could bestow upon a civilian. Among other honors were a life-size bronze plaque of McVey in the library and a faculty dinner at which the President was presented with a beautifully bound book containing 347 letters from friends all over the country. On May 28, 1940, the Lexington *Herald* carried a fourteen-page section filled with tributes to McVey and articles dealing with his accomplishments.

The *Kernel* in its tribute to the retiring President included his definition of a university which he had stated on more than one occasion:

> What is a university?
> A university is a place;
> It is a spirit:
> It is men of learning,
> A collection of books,
> Laboratories where work in science goes forward;
> It is the source of the teaching
> Of the beauties of literature and the arts;

It is the center where ambitious youth gathers to
   learn;
It protects the traditions,
Honors the new and tests its value;
It believes in truth,
Protests against error,
And leads men by reason
Rather than by force.

On June 7, 1940, McVey delivered the commencement
address to the graduating class. Both he and Mrs. McVey
were given honorary degrees.

Frank L. McVey's twenty-three years as President of the
University of Kentucky had come to an end. He had taken
a school which was a university in name and made it a
university in fact. His contributions in bricks and mortar
were obvious, but his real contribution went much deeper
than that. He had given to his faculty and even to some
of the students an understanding of the nature of a
university, of its place in society, and of the contributions
which it can and must make.

Contributions to the store of man's knowledge are not
often understood by undergraduates, but those who are
serious students appreciate the inspiration gained from
dedicated teachers. Those who attended the University
of Kentucky in the McVey period will always remember
Joseph W. Pryor in Anatomy and Physiology, Charles
Barkenbus in Chemistry, L. L. Dantzler and E. F. Far-
quhar in English, Adolph E. Bigge in German, Robert G.
Lunde and Ellery Hall in History, H. H. Downing and
Dudley South in Mathematics, Amry Vandenbosch and
Jasper Shannon in Political Science, William S. Webb,
Otto T. Koppius, and Louis Pardue in Physics, William D.
Funkhouser in Zoology, Walter S. Anderson, E. S. Good,
and J. Holmes Martin in Agriculture, Robert D. Haun,
R. D. McIntyre, and Rodman Sullivan in Commerce, John

S. Horine in Engineering, Leo M. Chamberlain in Education, and Roy Moreland in Law.[5]

Beginning on July 1, 1940, Thomas P. Cooper was handling four jobs at the University. In addition to being acting President, he was still Dean of the College of Agriculture, Director of the Experiment Station, and Director of Agricultural Extension. Experienced assistants in the last three positions made the handling of the new duties possible.

McVey on several occasions had to defend the University from attacks both from within and without. At least once during his acting presidency Cooper was required to do the same thing. One of the trustees whose intentions were good wished to scrutinize all candidates for the presidency carefully for any signs of radicalism. He also thought it would be good to screen all student applications to the University on the basis of their subscription to the American democracy and to extend such questioning to the faculty as well. Nothing, fortunately, really came of this issue.

Meanwhile the search for a President was continuing. Several board members thought that an answer had been found. They would give the job to Cooper on a permanent basis. When the board met in December, 1940, everything seemed settled, even to a press release on his selection to be handed to the newspapers at the close of the meeting. But Cooper refused to accept.

When the board met again on April 1, 1941, Judge Stoll, speaking for his four-member trustee committee, recommended that Dr. Herman L. Donovan, President of

5 Minutes of Board of Trustees, June 2, 1939, June 7, 1940; Minutes of University Senate, December 12, 1939; McVey Diary, 1938-1940, *passim;* Lexington *Leader,* January 7, 1939; Lexington *Herald,* April 4, May 28, 1940; Lexington *Herald-Leader,* October 1, 1939; Louisville *Courier-Journal,* July 12, 1939; *Kentucky Kernel,* May 28, 1940; Frances Jewell McVey (comp.), *A University Is a Place . . . A Spirit* (Lexington, 1944), p. 6.

Eastern Kentucky State Teachers College, be named President of the University of Kentucky. After some discussion, Donovan was elected unanimously.

The new President, who was to take office on July 1, 1941, was a native Kentuckian. He had attended Western Kentucky State Normal School from 1906 to 1908. After some experience as a teacher, he received his A.B. degree from State University in 1914. He had taken his M.A. at Columbia University and Ph.D. in Education at George Peabody College, with other graduate study at the University of Chicago. Donovan had been active in southern educational circles, and three years before his appointment to the presidency of the University of Kentucky, he had been elected president of the Southern Association of Colleges and Secondary Schools.

The board at its meeting on April 1, 1941, also made numerous changes in the organization of the University. The normal procedure would have been to ask acting President Cooper for recommendations or to wait until the new President took office on July 1 and allow him to make recommendations. The board did neither. It went into executive session, thus excluding Cooper and Business Agent D. H. Peak from the room. It was under these conditions that Donovan was elected. Cooper was not consulted in advance, nor was he present when the election took place.

While in executive session, the board took note of the fact that Peak would reach the age of seventy on May 27. A Department of Business Management and Control was created, headed by the Comptroller of the University, who would have broader powers than the previous business agent had possessed. He was charged with the "management and control of all finances, accounting, and operation of the several service departments, including, among others, the Department of Buildings and Grounds,

Student Union Building, all dining halls and cafeterias, all dormitories, the University Press, Campus Book Store, all publications of the University, the radio, and all other service departments of the University whether herein named or not." Frank Peterson, then director of the State Division of Accounts and Control in the administration of Governor Keen Johnson, was elected by the Board of Trustees to the new post of Comptroller of the University.

Next, the board created the office of Dean of the University, though they did not yet decide who should hold this position. He was charged with the management and general supervision of the office of Dean of Men, Dean of Women, the registrar, and the personnel of the library. Also he would have direct supervision of all academic personnel not specifically charged to the various colleges or departments of the University, or its graduate or summer school.

The most sweeping change was the replacement of the University Senate by a body called the Faculty of the University, but which consisted solely of administrators—the President, the comptroller, the Dean of the University, the deans of the several colleges, the Dean of the Graduate School, and the Director of the Summer School. This Faculty would be the "final authority of the University in all matters pertaining to the curricula and the recommending of the granting of degrees by the University, subject only to the Board of Trustees."

McVey had realized the Senate needed reorganizing, but he felt that a democratic type of internal organization could be maintained. Perhaps the size of the body could have been reduced by allowing the faculty members to elect as their representatives the members of a smaller Senate. The *Kernel* protested against the new organization. The Student Government Association called for a mass meeting of students, but no more than 120 attended.

This group passed a resolution asking the board to reconsider and to permit a joint Senate-Board committee to make a study of administration in other state universities. The University Senate met for the last time on June 4, 1941. It petitioned the board for a reconsideration of its recent action and pointed out that the trend in American colleges and universities was toward greater participation by the teaching staffs in policy making.

The minutes of the next meeting of the Board of Trustees, held on June 5, 1941, contain no reference to the student resolution or the petition of the Senate. The one-year Cooper administration had been in a large measure an extension of the McVey administration. On July 1, the new administration would go into effect. An era in the history of the University of Kentucky had come to an end.[6]

[6] R. P. Hobson to T. P. Cooper, December 17, 1940, January 11, 1941, Chamberlain to Cooper, January 4, 1941, Cooper to Hobson, January 8, 1941, University of Kentucky Archives; McVey Diary, December 15, 1939, January 11, April 1, 2, 4, 1941; Minutes of Board of Trustees, April 1, 1941; Minutes of University Senate, June 4, 1941; *Kentucky Kernel*, April 4, 11, 15, 25, 1941.

CHAPTER XI

THE WAR YEARS

BEFORE Herman L. Donovan had completed his first six months as President of the University of Kentucky, the United States was at war. Although the war effort necessarily absorbed many of the University's facilities, the new President was convinced that traditional courses of study should not be neglected. He reported to the Board of Trustees that while the University was ready to offer instruction to at least 3,000 men, yet this special training was only a temporary objective for an institution of higher education. The board must continue to think of the permanent values which a university renders to society. "Liberal education must not be permitted to languish," he continued. "Technical education may be essential to winning the war, but it is liberal education that will win the peace." Donovan's attitude may have helped to relieve the minds of some faculty members who had feared that as a result of his background and training, he would think of education as primarily vocational and would let the liberal arts be neglected.

In some ways the teaching services of the University were broadened during the war period. There were more late afternoon and evening classes, and forums dealing with war-related topics were conducted in surrounding towns. Two separate gifts of new radio receivers from Station WHAS made it possible to increase the number of mountain listening centers to more than seventy. Beginning in 1940 the University operated its own shortwave transmitter at the mountain town of Beattyville, and in

1944 it was granted permission to establish an FM station on the campus.

In the field of adult education the College of Arts and Sciences in 1942 inaugurated a series of four public lectures a year by outstanding professors elected by their colleagues in each of the four divisions of the college: Literature, Philosophy, and the Arts; Social Studies; Physical Sciences; and Biological Sciences. Three years later the plan for the Arts and Sciences lectures was modified. One lecturer was chosen, given the title of distinguished professor, and also freed from teaching duties for one quarter so that he might give full time to research and writing. Grant Knight of the Department of English held the first of these professorships. From time to time during the war years new degrees and new departments were established. In 1942 the Department of Romance Languages was authorized to offer work leading to the Ph.D., and the Department of Library Science, lately accredited by the American Library Association, was able to award the degree of B.S. in Library Science. In 1944 the Department of Psychology began to offer a training program in the field of industrial psychology, said at the time to have been one of the first of its kind in the country.

Donovan found three positions waiting to be filled when he took up his duties as President of the University. The new post of Dean of the University he turned over to Dr. Henry H. Hill, a former professor in the College of Education and former superintendent of schools in Lexington. After a year as Dean of the University, Hill resigned to become superintendent of schools at Pittsburgh. Dr. Leo M. Chamberlain, who had been registrar since 1937, was then appointed to fill the post of Dean of the University, but remained registrar as well. Later Donovan said of Chamberlain, "He was an incessant worker, calm in judgment, quiet in manner, and courageous when courage was needed." To the vacant position of Dean of Women he appointed Mrs. Sarah B. Holmes, who had served twelve years as assistant to Dean Sarah Blanding. Dean Blanding had resigned to head the School of Home Economics at Cornell. The new division of Maintenance and Operations, which had replaced the Department of Buildings and Grounds, was headed by Elgan Farris, who had been an associate professor of engineering.

In 1942 Dr. J. D. Williams, Director of the University Training School, resigned to accept the presidency of Marshall College and was replaced by Dr. Ellis Hartford. In the same year Dr. Herbert L. Riley was brought from the University of Washington to head the Botany Department. In 1944 a Department of Social Work was established under the chairmanship of Professor Harold Wetzel, and Dr. Joseph R. Schwendeman became the head of a new Department of Geography.[1]

President Donovan's formal inauguration was held on May 6, 1942, with more than two hundred colleges, universities, and learned societies sending delegates. At the end of the same month the University observed its seventy-fifth annual commencement by awarding more than the usual number of honorary degrees—a total of eighteen—to distinguished Kentuckians or former Kentuckians. In his inaugural address Donovan reminded his listeners that while the University must contribute all that it could to the war effort, it must not neglect its major mission. "We

[1] Minutes of Board of Trustees, September 15, December 11, 1941, May 29, 1942, January 12, 1943, April 4, September 23, 1944; Minutes of Executive Committee, June 19, 1942, May 17, August 20, 1943, February 25, July 21, 1944; McVey Diary, October 17, 1940; Minutes of Faculty, October 10, 1941, February 5, 1942; *Kentucky Kernel*, September 19, October 28, 1941, February 20, April 10, October 20, November 10, 1942, April 2, 1943, January 28, March 31, November 3, 1944, March 30, 1945; Lexington *Leader*, April 4, 1942; Lexington *Herald*, July 28, 1941; Louisville *Courier-Journal*, November 15, 1943, January 21, 1945; Herman Lee Donovan, *Keeping the University Free and Growing* (Lexington, 1959), pp. 8-9.

dare not permit the whirlwind that shakes the earth to blow out the lamp of learning, to extinguish the candle of culture. Education, like life, must go on; otherwise, chaos and the long night."[2] When this address was made, the University already was contributing to the war effort in manpower drawn from the faculty and the student body, in teaching, and in research. In the ROTC unit 1,145 men were in training. The College of Agriculture and Home Economics, as it was called at this time, was concentrating upon increasing food production in the state and upon the preservation of larger quantities of food. The Experiment Station was producing for the army a serum for the identification of paratyphoid bacteria. Many of the laboratories of the College of Engineering were engaged in war work, but none more completely than the aeronautical research laboratory.

At its meeting in May, 1942, the Board approved the establishment of a Signal Corps ROTC in addition to the infantry course already in effect. This program would commission twenty officers each year, and it was hoped that it would be continued after the war had ended. About the same time, the War Department announced a plan under which college students could join an Enlisted Reserve Corps and continue their education. These men were to be called to active duty before they had graduated only in case of dire necessity. But the situation changed, and very few of them remained to complete their education.

2 Louisville *Courier-Journal*, June 20, 1943, February 21, August 30, October 20, 1944; *Kentucky Kernel*, July 6, 1945; Lexington *Leader*, May 17, 1945; Lexington *Herald-Leader*, August 30, 1942, October 24, 1943; McVey Diary, May 6, 28, 1942; Minutes of Board of Trustees, April 7, May 9, 1942; Herman L. Donovan, "What I See from My Window," *The Educational Record*, XXIII (1942), 706; Minutes of Faculty, March 20, 1942.

In the fall of 1942 the University signed a contract to provide instruction for 870 soldiers in the College of Engineering. About the same time Donovan reported to the board that about 100 staff members had entered the armed forces; many more were serving the government in civilian capacities. Before this Engineers Specialist School closed in September, 1943, 3,174 soldiers had been trained.

By May, 1943, the Army Specialized Training Program was enrolling men in its program, and they began to arrive in Lexington. The engineering specialists were housed in the Phoenix Hotel downtown. Others were billeted in three men's dormitories and two of the women's dormitories on the campus. To furnish the longer and broader training which would be provided for ASTP men, it became necessary for the University to limit leaves of absence for faculty members to those who were actually drafted. Many of the faculty were teaching both civilians and soldiers. Often they worked in two departments, teaching, for example, botany to civilians and mathematics to soldiers. About sixty additional staff members had to be employed in order to handle properly the program that the University had undertaken.

In 1944 the number of ASTP trainees was gradually reduced, and faculty members had time for research, writing, and preparing for the expected influx of veterans when the war came to an end. A considerable amount of time was given to correspondence courses offered to military personnel through the United States Armed Forces Institute.

Despite the pressures of the war, the faculty of the University continued to be active in research. In the field of agriculture, experimentation with tobacco was moving ahead. Types resistant to more diseases and lower in nicotine content were being developed. Progress was made in the development of a hybrid, aromatic variety with some of the qualities of both Turkish and burley tobacco. Chemists at the Experiment Station were discovering new byproducts, many of which could be made from hitherto useless portions of the tobacco plant. In 1943 the College of Engineering established a Bureau of Engineering Research and Development to coordinate the research work in engineering. The Bureau of School Service, under Dr. Maurice Seay, was continuing the project on the effect of instructional materials upon the improvement of living conditions in rural communities. This experiment attracted interested observers from a number of other states.

Two large steps were taken toward the encouragement of research during the war years. One of these was the recommendation by the Haggin Publications Committee for the establishment of a University of Kentucky Press. In September, 1943, the Board of Trustees gave its approval, though no full-time staff was set up at that time. The second was the incorporation of the Kentucky Research Foundation in 1945 by four professors of the University, W. S. Webb, E. N. Fergus, C. C. Ross, and Frank Murray. Though not a part of the University, the research foundation was closely associated with it, for the President, the dean, and the comptroller were ex officio members of the board of directors and most of the other directors would come from the faculty and the University's trustees. The foundation solicited gifts for fellowships, scholarships, and for specific research projects; although applied research predominated in these projects, pure research was not ignored.[3]

[3] Minutes of Faculty, December 17, 1941, January 9, 17, February 5, 1942, February 21, 1944; Minutes of Board of Trustees, December 11, 1941, May 29, September 15, 1942, September 21, 1943; Minutes of Executive Committee, May 16, 1941, February 20, 1942, June 25, August 20, 1943, July 21, 1944; Lexington *Herald*, June 11, 1942, August 29, 1943; Lexington *Leader*, December 23, 1942; Donovan, *Keeping the University Free and Growing*, pp. 58-59.

As President of the University, Donovan never missed a chance to tell the public about the financial needs of the institution. He constantly compared Kentucky's appropriations for her University with those of other states. Sometimes he used as an example the state of Minnesota, which then had about the same population as Kentucky but gave six times as much to its state university. In September he told the Board of Trustees that the total amount appropriated by the General Assembly for University buildings during the seventy-five-year history of the institution did not exceed $1,300,000.

Before the Reorganization Act of 1934 the President and trustees could spend the University's appropriations as they thought wise. By careful management McVey's administration had been able to save out of operating expenses money which from time to time enabled them to erect buildings. During the last few years federal funds had been available for the erection of buildings, but this money covered only a part of the cost. The remainder was raised by issuing bonds, which would be retired with money collected in the form of student fees, dormitory rentals, and sales of food. These methods of financing placed an unfair share of the burden upon the parents of students who attended the University and allowed the citizens of Kentucky to remain secure in the commonly held belief that education was of value only to those who received it and not to society as a whole.

The 1942 General Assembly gave the University the largest increase in appropriations in the school's history up to that time. Money granted by the state for the 1942-1944 biennium amounted to $3,145,752, out of a total University income of $9,540,375. This enabled Donovan to put some members of the faculty on a twelve-month instead of a ten-month basis. The financial situation had improved, but much remained to be done.

When the board met in December, 1943, he presented the budget request for the 1944-1946 biennium and also called attention to a pamphlet which had been prepared for distribution throughout the state. This showed, by means of charts and graphs, that the University was receiving a smaller state appropriation than were the universities of any of the seven states which border Kentucky. When this was stated in terms of appropriation per student, Kentucky still ranked next to last. Nevertheless, the state appropriation for the 1944-1946 biennium was slightly less than for the preceding one, $3,008,571 out of a total income of $9,325,143.

The growing total income of the University was accounted for by gradually increasing federal funds and by restricted funds, such as the Haggin and Keeneland gifts and grants from foundations. The Keeneland Racetrack near Lexington was operated on a nonprofit basis. In 1941, its operator, the Keeneland Association, began to make gifts to the University. In 1944 it organized an affiliate, the Keeneland Foundation, to "conduct, promote, foster, and encourage experiments, research, studies, and investigations designed to extend and increase the field of scientific knowledge." Future aid to the University came from the foundation rather than from the association.

Donovan frequently reminded the board and state officials that the summer session, now called the summer quarter, was a part of the University year from an administrative point of view, though adequate financial provision had not been made for it. The position of Director of the Summer Session had been abolished, and the individual deans were responsible for the courses offered in their departments. Although some professors had been placed on a twelve-month basis and were available for teaching in the summer quarter, there were not nearly enough of such professors available. The pay of others who taught came from fees and from $10,000 per year appropriated by the legislature. Often the administration had to bargain with a teacher to teach a small group of students for a mere pittance in order to carry on the work of the summer quarter. This situation was not remedied until a special legislative session called by Governor Simeon Willis in the spring of 1944 made the necessary appropriation. From that time on all faculty members above the rank of instructor were on a twelve-month basis unless they requested otherwise.

So as to allow students to finish their college work a year earlier, the Executive Committee of the board had approved a change to the quarter system in June, 1942. The University remained on the quarter system until the summer of 1948, when it returned to a year of two semesters, with an eight-week summer term counting as half a semester.

In 1942 the Court of Appeals held that the $5,000 salary limitation in Kentucky's constitution applied to state employees as well as to elected officials. This would include professors and administrative officers of the University. A constitutional amendment designed to remove this restriction from the salaries of employees and of judges of the Court of Appeals was submitted to the voters in 1943 and overwhelmingly defeated. This defeat made it even more difficult to find replacements for those faculty members who had resigned.

In the following year Attorney General Eldon S. Dummit held, as had his predecessor, that money in the Haggin and Keeneland funds could be used to supplement salaries. Thus those few who were above the $5,000 limit continued to draw that amount from public funds and the balance of their salaries from these restricted funds. So long as the cost of living remained at a point where very few salaries had to exceed the constitutional limit, this system worked well. There is no doubt that some members of the staff who could have commanded higher salaries elsewhere remained out of loyalty to Kentucky and its University. One of these was Donovan himself, who in 1945 was offered the presidency of Peabody College at a higher salary than he was receiving at the time.

As might have been expected, the University's enrollment showed a continual decline during the war years. In 1941-1942 the registration figures show a total of 5,145. The figure dropped to 4,168 in 1942-1943, to 3,213 in 1943-1944, and to 3,156 in 1944-1945.

Very little building was done on the campus while the war was in progress. A Highway Research Laboratory was completed in 1941, a Coal Research Laboratory in 1943, and an Animal Pathology Building in 1945. There was much talk of a fieldhouse, and some property for a site was acquired, but actual construction would have to wait until peace came.

When Donovan was chosen as President, he did not know that the University Senate had been abolished and with it the faculty share in the making of University policies. Donovan said later that if he had known this fact, he probably would not have accepted the position. As soon as possible, the new President asked Dr. Jesse E. Adams of the College of Education to make a study of the organization of sixty-two universities. Based upon this study, which took a long time to make, Donovan presented to the board, September 15, 1942, several possible plans for returning to the faculty a share in policy making. The board granted Donovan the authority to appoint a committee to study the matter further. This became known as the Committee of Fifteen, and Dean Cooper served as its chairman. It was to study the question and make recommendations for another reorganization at Kentucky.

When presented, the plan of the Committee of Fifteen

HERMAN LEE DONOVAN

called for a policy-making body to be known as the University Faculty. Ex officio members would be the President of the University, the Dean of the University, the Dean of the Graduate School, the deans of the colleges, the Dean of Men, the Dean of Women, the registrar, the comptroller, the Director of Extension, the librarian, and the president of the Student Government Association. There would be forty elected members of the rank of assistant professor or above who would serve three-year terms with one-third retiring each year. Seven members were to be chosen from Literature, Philosophy, and the Arts, three from Social Studies, four from Physical Sciences, four from Biological Sciences, one from Athletics, one from Military Science, seven from Agriculture, one from Home Economics, five from Engineering, one from Law, three from Education, and three from Commerce. The representative from Military Science and Tactics later was made an ex officio member, leaving thirty-nine elected members.

The board, which on April 1, 1941, had created a so-called Faculty consisting of administrators, was not favorable to the new organization when Donovan presented it to them. Obviously if it came to a vote, it would be turned down. The President withdrew the proposal. Before the next meeting of the board, he talked to individual members about the matter. On April 6, 1943, he presented the plan again, explaining that the lack of democracy in the existing organization might incur the disfavor of accrediting agencies and the ridicule of other universities. This time the Committee of Fifteen's plan was adopted unanimously. The President gave to this committee the further duty of revising the Governing Regulations of the University to bring them into harmony with the new organization.

When the new Faculty met for the first time on

October 11, 1943, Donovan said to them: "This is an historic event. . . . No group of men and women that has ever assembled on our campus had greater responsibility toward the future development of the University. . . . You are not here to represent your department or your college, but you are here to represent the University. I hope that the problems that will come before you from time to time will be discussed by you as a member of the University, and not from the standpoint of how they may possibly affect any department or college."

As a means of recognizing and encouraging scholarship, the University in 1945 held its first annual Honors Day convocation. At this time students who had been elected to honor societies, who had received fellowships or scholarships, or who had made a cumulative standing of 2.3 or better were given special recognition.

In 1944 the Executive Committee of the board, on Donovan's recommendation, designated February 22 as Founders Day. It was on that date in 1865 that the General Assembly had passed an act establishing the Agricultural and Mechanical College of Kentucky which eventually became the University of Kentucky. The day was celebrated for the first time on February 22, 1945, with President Emeritus McVey and Governor Simeon Willis as the principal speakers.[4]

In the early years of his administration President Donovan was concerned over the large number of students who dropped out of the University before graduation. To study this problem he appointed a committee, with

4 Donovan, *Keeping the University Free and Growing*, pp. 2-4, 19-20; Minutes of Board of Trustees, September 16, 1941, April 7, September 15, 1942, January 12, April 6, December 14, 1943, April 4, September 23, 1944; Minutes of Executive Committee, October 11, 1941, February 20, 1942, January 21, April 4, July 21, 1944, May 22, 1947; *The University of Kentucky: Its History and Development*, pp. 22, 31; McVey Diary, February 2, 22, May 14, 1945; *Kentucky Kernel*, April 16, 1943, May 4, 1945, August 5, 1951; Minutes of the Faculty, October 11, 1943, August 24, 1944.

Dr. Martin M. White, Assistant Dean of the College of Arts and Sciences as its chairman. This committee presented a very thoughtful report to the Faculty. "The colleges of the University," said the report, "have certain common objectives for the freshman year, one of which is to prepare the student effectively for advanced or professional study. . . . The majority of freshmen entering the University, however, do not remain to pursue either advanced or professional courses." The report then concluded that for this large number of students the present course offerings for freshmen were not the best the faculty could devise.

Although the committee realized that some of the colleges provided advisers for freshmen, it felt that this advisory work was seldom recognized by reduction in the teaching load or increase in pay. As a result, they gave little time to their advisees, many of whom left the University without anyone knowing what their difficulties had been.

It was felt, too, that very little had been done to provide general or vocational education for those who did not succeed in the regular curricula. In some cases students dropped out of school not because of lack of ability or preparation for college work, but because they had gotten into fields which were wrong for them, and no one had helped them to find themselves.

The committee then recommended the establishment of a University College which would have its own dean and an advisory committee to assign students to counselors. The committee would enroll in the University College all freshmen, sophomores on scholastic probation, and certain junior and senior transfers. It was expected that freshmen would spend three quarters in the University College and complete the course requirement. There would be two-year curricula also for those students who did not care to work toward degrees. Diplomas would be awarded to all who finished a two-year program. After several months of study and spirited debate, the plan for a University College was dropped. President Donovan concurred with this decision, but suggested that the aims be achieved within the existing framework of the institution within a reasonable time. He suggested also that the individual colleges adjust their curricula to the needs of more students and that they consider the advisability of terminal courses for those students who do not have the ability or inclination to pursue more than two years of college work. He thought that vocational courses might well be considered in the Colleges of Agriculture, Commerce, and Arts and Sciences. He thought, too, that all of the colleges should consider the problem of a broader base, with a view to having their graduates more liberally educated when they completed their work for a degree.

Although the major sports were affected by the shortage of physically fit male students available during the war, Kentucky missed only one year of football and managed to have a basketball team every year. Football coach Ab Kirwan never had a championship team, but he escaped most of the bitter feeling which students and other fans had directed toward previous coaches. In 1942 tackle Clyde Johnson attracted enough attention to be named on the Associated Press's All-American team. This was an honor that had been won by several Kentucky basketball players, but in football Johnson was the first. Although football was in a sense a war casualty, Coach Rupp's basketball teams continued their winning ways, winning three Southeastern Conference championships.[5]

[5] Minutes of the Faculty, November 27, 1942, February 23, October 11, December 13, 1943, February 14, 21, November 13, December 11, 1944; Minutes of Board of Trustees, May 29, 1942; Minutes of Executive Committee, February 17, 1945; *Kentucky Kernel,* March 14, 1939, September 19, October 10, 1941, January 6, April 28, October 30, 1942, January 8, July 2, October 15, 22, 1943, October 27, 1944.

Although much of his energies had naturally to be devoted to the special problems of the University in wartime, President Donovan showed during the first years of his presidency that he was prepared to carry on the leadership shown by the McVey administration. He stressed the value of the liberal arts and the University's role in maintaining such studies even in wartime. And he was successful in restoring to the faculty a voice in making policy for the University. A possible obstacle to the future growth of the University's faculty was the Court of Appeals ruling that the $5,000 salary limitation applied to employees of the state as well as to elected officials. Fortunately it was decided that funds from the Haggin and Keeneland gifts could be used to supplement salaries at the University. The limitation, nevertheless, created a problem that would have to be reckoned with in the future.

CHAPTER XII

KEEPING THE UNIVERSITY FREE

ANY PUBLIC INSTITUTION is subject to pressures from people or from groups who, sometimes from the most commendable motives, wish it to do this or that. A university with its claim for academic freedom to search out and disseminate the truth is perhaps more sensitive to such pressures than other institutions and must the more zealously protect itself against any encroachment upon its liberties. The burden of this falls most heavily upon the university's president, but if he is to be successful, he must have the support of public officials and, finally, of the public itself.

President McVey had earlier withstood such an attack in the controversy over the teaching of evolution in the public schools. During his administration he had to contend with numerous others, some of them trivial, but all requiring tact and firmness in their handling. Some businessmen, for example, thought that they should be getting more business from the University, and two utilities companies believed that they were being criticized unfairly by some of the faculty. Once McVey was summoned to appear before the Fayette County Grand Jury, where he was informed of the connection of two faculty members with a strike during the construction of the mansion at Spindletop Farm. Every so often the accusation of radicalism would be brought up by some citizen. McVey was able to ward off all these attacks without there being any serious threats to the University.

Donovan, too, had to contend with forces that were exerted against the University. After his retirement he

wrote that this had been one of the most serious problems
that he had faced. Probably the most threatening of these
forces was the gradual encroachment of the state upon
University affairs, a problem common to many state universities and colleges. In Kentucky this happened gradually. For example, in 1934, an act was passed which gave
the Governor the authority to remove members of any
and all state boards, including the Board of Trustees of
the University, without bringing any charges or giving any
reason for doing so. In 1936 the state adopted the principle of the executive budget. Instead of presenting its
needs to a committee of the legislature, the University was
required to present them to the Department of Finance.
Here the proposed budget could be cut at the will of the
executive branch. By 1948 a State Building Commission
could approve or disapprove the construction of buildings
at the University and other state institutions. No longer
would the trustees have the last word on the President's
recommendations regarding needed buildings. In the
same year the legislature, upon the recommendation of the
Governor, reduced the terms of members of the board
from six years to four years, bringing the terms of the
twelve appointed members in line with those of the three
ex officio members, but also giving the Governor the
opportunity to appoint an entire board. Against this
measure Donovan protested to Governor Earle Clements
without success.

In 1950 a more serious piece of legislation was passed.
The Division of Personnel in the Department of Finance
was given control over the salaries of employees of the
University, with the Governor having the final word. In
March of that year Donovan and representatives of the
state colleges met with the Governor and explained to
him the danger of this legislation. It would, they pointed
out, give the chief executive of the state control over the

institutions of higher learning. Donovan also explained to the trustees the seriousness of the situation and warned them that it might affect the University's accreditation. The Board of Trustees requested the Governor and the legislature to restore its "authority to classify positions, and fix salaries of all professors and other employees." It was obvious that requesting would not be sufficient. Already Donovan had sought the help of the Southern Association of Colleges and Secondary Schools, the American Association of Colleges for Teacher Education, and the University of Kentucky chapter of the American Association of University Professors.

The Southern Association, meeting in Richmond, Virginia, approved the following statement: "The Association views with grave concern the enactment of certain statutes of the General Assembly of 1950 duly signed by the Governor of the Commonwealth of Kentucky. These statutory provisions are now the law and deprive the Board of Trustees and Regents of their control of the institutions of higher learning by taking from them their power and authority to administer the affairs of their institutions. Such legislation is a violation of the declaration of principles announced by the Southern Association of Colleges and Secondary Schools and is in conflict with its Constitution and standards. Under such legislation the membership of the Kentucky state colleges and of the University of Kentucky in the Association is in jeopardy, and the Executive Secretary of the Commission on Institutions of Higher Education will so inform the president of the affected member institutions."

The American Association of Colleges for Teacher Education passed a similar resolution. The Kentucky AAUP chapter studied the question carefully and published at its own expense a sixty-page pamphlet entitled, "Relations Between the State Government and the University of Kentucky." Allan M. Trout of the *Courier-Journal* called this a "declaration of independence."

Upon the recommendation of Governor Lawrence Wetherby, the 1952 legislature came to the rescue of the University on the major issue. An act was passed which stated that: "Anything in any statutes of the Commonwealth to the contrary notwithstanding, the power over and control of appointments, qualifications, salaries, and compensation payable out of the state treasury or otherwise, promotions, and official relations of all employees of the University of Kentucky . . . shall be under the exclusive jurisdiction of the Board of Trustees of the University of Kentucky, which shall be an independent agency and instrumentality of the Commonwealth." A similar statement was applied to the state colleges. This legislation removed the University and the state colleges from control by the Division of Personnel. It also removed the University, but not the colleges, from the State Department of Education, where it had been since 1934.[1]

Another instance of pressure occurred when Dean Cooper of the College of Agriculture reached the age of seventy in the spring of 1951 and was due for retirement. Donovan wished to secure the best possible man for the position and had been assured by Hal Price Headley of the Keeneland Foundation that the foundation would give any necessary help on the matter of salary.

The Louisville *Courier-Journal* and other newspapers

[1] Donovan, *Keeping the University Free and Growing*, 71-72; McVey, *The Gates Open Slowly*, 284-85; McVey Diary, February 5, March 20, 1948; Louisville *Courier-Journal*, June 17, 1951; Donovan to Clements, February 11, 1948, Donovan to Charles W. Hunt, December 13, 1950, J. M. Godard to Donovan, December 13, 1950, Donovan to Godard, December 18, 1950, Charles W. Hunt to Donovan, February 21, 1951, Donovan to Board, December 19, 1951, Donovan to Godard, March 5, 1952, Donovan to Albert J. Geiger, March 5, 1952, Donovan's Memorandum of Board Action, December 12, 1950, Donovan Papers; Minutes of Executive Committee, January 21, 1949.

warned, however, that a political appointment was being planned for Dean Cooper's successor. Such rumors were persistent. They continued to appear in newspapers, and they also came to Donovan in conversations with persons who were worried about the possibility of political interference in the affairs of the University. Members of the board admitted that they were under great pressure. Donovan sent editorials and other newspaper clippings to the secretary-treasurer of the American Association of Colleges for Teacher Education and requested that the association take a firm stand on the issue.

The President was encouraged by a resolution passed by the Kentucky Farm Bureau strongly condemning political interference in the selection of a dean, and he felt that the trustees would withstand the pressure on them. When the board met in April, 1951, Donovan recommended Dr. Frank J. Welch, Dean of the School of Agriculture at Mississippi State College and Director of the Mississippi Experiment Station, and the board approved his recommendation. The new dean was a graduate of the University of Colorado, had done his doctoral work at the University of Wisconsin, and had served with distinction in several government posts. For the good outcome of this situation, Donovan gave much of the credit to the newspapers and the support of the public which they had rallied.[2]

One of the most difficult problems encountered by

2 Louisville *Courier-Journal*, January 6, 11, 28, February 20, April 5, 18, 1951; Lexington *Herald*, March 8, 21, 1951; McVey Diary, April 3, 1951; Minutes of Board of Trustees, April 3, 1951; W. S. Anderson to Donovan, January 11, 1951, Donovan to Anderson, January 15, 1951, Donovan to Charles W. Hunt, January 16, 1951, J. Lindsay Nunn to B. C. Cotton, January 19, 1951, Donovan to Marshall Barnes, January 22, 1951, Lee Sprowles to Eugene F. Bradford, January 24, 1951, Donovan to Russell L. Thackrey, April 16, 1951, Resolution of Kentucky Farm Bureau Federation, February 21, 1951, Memorandum of Conversation with Hal Price Headley, October 16, 1950, Donovan Papers.

President Donovan during his administration was a series of incidents over the Wenner-Gren Aeronautical Research Laboratory, which involved Colonel Graham, the Dean of the College of Engineering. Early in 1942 the name of Axel Wenner-Gren was listed by the State Department among those whose assets were blocked for the duration of the war; as a result, suspicions were directed at the laboratory and at Graham, who had been responsible for securing it from Wenner-Gren. Graham's situation was further complicated by his accepting a consultative post in Washington while retaining the deanship of the Engineering College. Finally a suit was brought against him to recover the salary which had been paid him by the state; the suit charged that he had rendered no services to the University since beginning his work in Washington. Though this suit was dismissed by a local court and later by the Kentucky Court of Appeals, a petition was sent the Governor asking for an investigation of the Wenner-Gren Laboratory; the Governor's request for a report was answered in a pamphlet prepared by Dr. Leo Chamberlain, which showed that there was nothing at all suspicious in the operation of the laboratory, though in response to earlier petitions President Donovan had removed Wenner-Gren's name from the building until the outcome of his case could be determined by the State Department. Even the money still owed the faculty from the 1931-1932 school year was eventually brought into the controversy. Finally the disagreements culminated in a resolution introduced in the legislature in 1946 calling for an investigation of the University. The legislative committee gave Donovan a unanimous vote of confidence. In June of the same year Dean Graham's request for change-of-work status was approved by the Board of Trustees, and thus a controversy that had dragged out through the war years was brought to its close.

Throughout the controversy President Donovan, on the one hand, attempted to counter the suspicions and charges directed toward the Wenner-Gren Laboratory, charges for which no evidence was ever found, and after the war the name of Wenner-Gren was cleared by the State Department and his name restored to the building. On the other hand, Donovan defended Dean Graham. To the trustees he pointed out that Graham's work in Washington had been helpful in the matter of gaining government contracts for the University and that he had kept up his administrative duties at the University. To others he stated his belief that such attacks upon one member of the faculty constituted a danger to everyone and should be resisted forcefully, for if the attacks proved successful, then anyone might be subject to them and no member of the faculty could consider himself safe.[3]

Other situations also arose during Donovan's administration such as any university president must face at some time during his career. One parent objected to a book which his daughter had been assigned to read in her freshman English class. A politician tried to secure a part-time teaching job for a friend. A candidate for Governor objected to an article in the University Extension Bulletin that urged the people to support calling a convention to

[3] Minutes of Executive Committee, December 14, 1937, February 25, May 2, June 13, 1944, February 15, May 25, 26, 1946; McVey Diary, 1937-1946, *passim;* Minutes of Board of Trustees, April 5, June 3, 1938, September 19, 1939, April 4, June 2, 1944, April 3, May 28, 1945, April 2, June 4, July 19, 1946; Minutes of Faculty, May 8, 1944; Donovan, *Keeping the University Free and Growing,* 72-75; *Kentucky Kernel,* April 7, 28, 1944, April 13, 1945, March 29, 1946; R. C. Stoll to Cordell Hull, January 25, 1943, Donovan to Marshall Barnes, March 27, 1944, Donovan to Alexander Capurso, April 5, 8, 1944, Donovan to Harper Gatton, April 8, 1944, Donovan to Stoll, November 25, 1944, August 25, 1945, Donovan to R. P. Hobson, July 7, 1944, August 20, September 20, 1945, M. M. White to Donovan, March 9, 1945, White to Leo M. Chamberlain, April 20, 1945, Donovan Papers; Julius H. Amberg to A. B. Chandler, April 28, 1944, in *The Facts* (Bulletin of the University of Kentucky), pp. 27-28.

revise the state constitution. Donovan's response to such situations varied as the occasion seemed to demand, but always he maintained the University's duty to be a "forum where every point of view can be expressed so far as it is not inconsistent with the principles of democracy." Nor can it be doubted that his firmness did much to sustain the University's integrity, and in this he received McVey's approbation.

CHAPTER XIII

THE POSTWAR YEARS

THE PERIOD following the close of World War II was a unique one in the experience of American schools and colleges. Near the end of the war, Congress had enacted Public Law 346, better known as the G. I. Bill, which provided financial assistance to eligible veterans who wished to continue their education or training. Beginning in June, 1944, when the program went into effect, veterans by the thousands crowded into colleges over the United States. To the colleges this sudden swarm of students was a welcome, but sometimes harassing, problem; added classroom space had somehow to be found, housing had to be manufactured, and faculty secured to teach the swelling classes. The country as a whole felt a tremendous upsurge after the austerities of wartime; people everywhere were seeking greater opportunities. The University participated in all this, and in the challenges that were posed.

At the University the most obvious change in the early years after the war was the increase in enrollment. From a little over 3,000 in 1944-1945, the enrollment climbed to 6,105 in the next academic year. Thereafter it rose steadily, reaching a high of 10,213 in 1949-1950.

The University's income from all sources increased after the war, although its total income remained below the average for state universities. For the 1946-1948 biennium the state appropriated $4,579,544 out of a total income of $15,548,065. For the 1948-1950 biennium the institution's total income was $17,894,494 of which the state contributed $6,293,083. The growing difference between the state appropriations to the University and its total income reflects in part the increases in federal funds and in restricted funds contributed for specific purposes by individuals, corporations, and foundations. The type of revenue which showed the greatest increase, however, was that coming as a consequence of the inflated postwar enrollments.

Although more classrooms and laboratories were needed to handle the increased enrollment, the immediate necessity was in housing. Fortunately, surplus prefabricated houses were available. Two hundred were obtained at Charlestown, Indiana, and 124 more from Willow Run, Michigan. The cost, including furnishings, was only five dollars per unit, but the University had to transport them to Lexington and construct roads and utilities for them. In this way Cooperstown on the north end of the Experiment Station Farm came into being. This housing was available only to married veterans, and the population of the village at its maximum was close to 1,000.

At the southwest corner of the farm Shawneetown, another housing project, was built by the federal government. Restricted to veterans with children, it contained 182 units in barracks-type buildings. A few buildings in each village were reserved for faculty members. Barracks for single veterans were also constructed and provided space for 326 men and 48 women. Several houses near the University were leased or purchased for additional living quarters for women students, and dormitory space was leased at the Sayre School about a mile north of the campus. Residents of Lexington who had never rented rooms before were urged to open their homes to students, and many did so.

To provide the needed classrooms it was necessary to erect temporary buildings and to make use of houses owned by the University. This group included a building for the social sciences, a chemistry laboratory, an engineering annex, and a cafeteria. Some of these temporary buildings achieved a surprising permanence.

Buildings of a permanent nature were planned and some were started, but only three were completed in the 1940s. The largest of these was a dormitory for men located on Washington Avenue. It completed a quadrangle, the other three sides of which were formed by Bradley, Kinkead, and Breckinridge halls. The new Dormitory was named Bowman Hall in honor of John B. Bowman, regent of Kentucky University, of which the Agricultural and Mechanical College of Kentucky had been a part from 1865 to 1878. The other two permanent structures were an addition to the Animal Pathology Building and a Dairy Center.

In a period when the University needed all available space it was struck by three fires in consecutive years. On February 15, 1946, the converted tobacco warehouse housing the Department of Maintenance and Operations and the Department of Physical Education was completely destroyed. The loss included supplies, trucks, tools, and machines, and practically all of the unsold copies of books published by the University Press. As quickly as possible plans were made for a three-story service building with the third floor to be used for library storage, but in the meantime a temporary building had to be erected on the farm. On February 10, 1947, the frame building on Euclid Avenue which was used by the Music Department and the Guignol Theater burned. Plans for a new Fine Arts Building were being considered; again a temporary building had to be erected to solve the immediate problem. Before daybreak on the morning of November 12, 1948, fire broke out in Norwood Hall, which housed the Department of Botany, and it too was a total loss. Destroyed with the building were laboratory equipment and a herbarium that had been assembled over a long period of years.

During this period, when dormitories, classrooms, and

laboratories were badly needed, a beginning was made on a building which many felt had been given too high a priority. Before the war the existing gymnasium could no longer accommodate the crowds that wanted to see Kentucky's basketball teams in action, and in 1942 through an appropriation from the legislature land at the corner of Euclid and Lexington avenues was acquired and cleared as a site for a fieldhouse. The war prevented any further action.

The 1946 legislature made an appropriation for the building, but no start was made that year. In 1947 contracts were let for excavation, foundation, and structural steel work. The 1948 legislature made an additional appropriation which was believed at the time to be enough to complete the building. Donovan succeeded in having plans drawn for a building which would be more than a gymnasium. It was his intention to have it serve also as an auditorium where lectures might be given, and commencements and convocations held. When the cornerstone was laid on February 22, 1949, Kentuckians, through their representatives, had sanctioned the spending of more than $3,000,000 on the building. In April of that year the board decided that it would be called Memorial Coliseum in honor of those Kentuckians who gave their lives in World War II. Before the building could be finished, almost another $1,000,000 had to be raised by the selling of bonds. The Athletic Association expected to retire these with money collected for admission to games. At the same time the football stadium was being doubled in size, the cost to be met in the same way.

Other buildings planned at this time and under construction before the end of the decade were a Journalism Building and an addition to the central heating plant. Three buildings which had been known only by the uses to which they were put were now given names. The Engineering Building was named for Dean Anderson, the Biological Sciences Building for Dean Funkhouser, and the Training School for Dean Taylor.[1]

From the end of the war to the close of the forties the faculty at the University went through a number of changes. Schools over the country were looking for additional instructors, and the University, which could not compete with the salaries offered by many other institutions, lost many staff members who took better paying jobs elsewhere. Six of the vacancies which occurred were in administrative posts; the Dean of Men and the Deans of Arts and Sciences, Law, Commerce, and Engineering all retired, and Dean Taylor of the College of Education died. For two of these posts President Donovan selected surprisingly young men. Elvis Stahr came to the University in 1947 and now, a year later, became Dean of the College of Law, while Frank G. Dickey, who had received his Ed.D. from the University in 1947, was named first acting Dean and then shortly afterward, in 1949, Dean of the College of Education. To find the new Deans of Commerce and of Arts and Sciences, Donovan canvassed the two colleges, and on the basis of his inquiries Martin M. White was made Dean of Arts and Sciences and Cecil Carpenter took over the College of Commerce. To replace Colonel Graham of Engineering, D. V. Terrell moved up from his position as head of the Department of Civil Engineering. A. D. Kirwan, who had taken leave of absence as football coach in 1945 to earn his doctorate in

[1] Minutes of Board of Trustees, June 4, September 21, December 10, 1946, February 25, April 1, June 3, December 16, 1947, May 3, June 25, August 9, December 18, 1948, April 5, September 20, December 13, 1949; *The University of Kentucky: Its History and Development,* pp. 7, 22, 31; Donovan, *Keeping the University Free and Growing,* pp. 30-31, 34-35; *Kentucky Kernel,* February 11, 25, 1949; Minutes of Executive Committee, October 17, 1945, February 15, March 5, May 25, August 23, 1946, January 24, 1947, May 24, 1948, May 11, October 15, November 19, 1949.

history at Duke, returned in 1947 and assumed T. T. Jones' duties as Dean of Men.

In 1946 Donovan recommended that the position of Vice President be created. Dr. Chamberlain was named to this post, and he was replaced as Dean of the University and Registrar by Dr. Maurice Seay of the College of Education. Three years afterward, the latter position was divided. Seay continued as Dean of the University, and Lee Sprowles, also from the College of Education, became Registrar.

A number of departments also needed administrative appointments during this period. In Engineering, E. B. Penrod assumed direction of the Department of Mechanical Engineering while R. E. Shaver moved into Dean Terrell's former place in Civil Engineering. Other new department heads were Edwin Stein in Music, Don Cash Seaton in Physical Education, and Herman E. Spivey in English.[2]

The administration, perhaps prompted by the increasing competition in securing and holding good men, created a new academic rank in 1948. This was called distinguished professor and carried with it an increase in salary. At the beginning, seven members of the faculty were given this rank; they were Thomas D. Clark, Amry Vandenbosch, Grant Knight, and Louis Pardue from Arts and Sciences, James W. Martin from Commerce, and William D. Valleau and Philip R. Edwards from Agriculture. In the next year Herbert Sorenson from Education was added

2 Minutes of Executive Committee, February 15, May 25, August 23, November 15, 1946, May 22, July 18, August 28, 1947, July 16, 1948; *Kentucky Kernel,* June 27, July 17, 1947; McVey Diary, February 14, 1947, February 15, 1948; Lexington *Leader,* January 23, 1946; Lexington *Herald-Leader,* August 25, 1946, September 25, 1949; Edward Wiest to Donovan, July 16, 1946, May 31, 1948, Donovan Papers; Minutes of Board of Trustees, September 18, 1945, June 4, September 21, 1946, February 25, April 1, June 3, 1947, May 3, June 25, September 15, 1948, December 13, 1949.

to this group. The College of Arts and Sciences continued its recognition of outstanding faculty members in the annual selection of Distinguished Professor of the Year, an honor which allowed freed time for research.

The advancing reputation and maturity of the University's faculty could be seen in the growing number of those who were asked to serve as visiting professors or as consultants. Serving in this capacity were, among others, Arthur C. McFarlan who lectured at Columbia, Clement Eaton at Princeton and the University of Wisconsin, and Thomas D. Clark at the Salzburg Seminar in American Civilization. President Donovan went to Germany for the War Department as a consultant on university organization.[3]

Research and publication were also carried on at an increasing rate. From 1944 to 1948 faculty members produced some 35 books, 220 bulletins and pamphlets, and 585 articles. The Kentucky Research Foundation, created in 1946, secured and administered funds for research projects. In 1948 the legislature began appropriating money for the advancement of research; a University committee was set up to administer these funds. Aid came to the area of the sciences from a gift of an electron microscope from the Keeneland Foundation, and in 1947 the University joined the Oak Ridge Institute of Nuclear Studies. A year later, through the aid of the Haggin Fund, the editorial offices of the *Journal of Southern History* were moved to Lexington, and Thomas D. Clark became the managing editor with Merton England as editorial associate.

[3] Minutes of Board of Trustees, June 4, September 21, 1946, September 27, December 16, 1947, February 14, May 3, 1948, June 3, July 1, 1949; Louisville *Courier-Journal*, April 13, 1949; Lexington *Leader*, July 24, 1947, October 11, 1948; Lexington *Herald-Leader*, July 25, 1948; *Kentucky Kernel*, 1945-1949, *passim;* Minutes of Faculty, October 15, 1945; Minutes of Executive Committee, January 19, 1946, January 24, November 21, 1947, March 16, November 6, 1948, March 22, 1949.

The library and museum resources of the University were likewise growing. Following the death of Dr. Funkhouser, his outstanding membracidae collection was given to the school by Mrs. Funkhouser. Judge Samuel M. Wilson of Lexington, always a friend of the University, bequeathed his collection of books, pamphlets, manuscripts, and maps to the library. Of the nearly 10,000 books in the collection, at least 1,000 were very rare. Pertaining largely to Kentucky and the Ohio Valley, this collection greatly strengthened the library's research facilities.

In 1948 Dr. Lawrence S. Thompson was employed as Director of Libraries for the University. Miss Margaret I. King remained as his assistant until she went on a change-of-work status a year later. After her retirement, the library building was named in her honor.[4]

On June 26, 1949, a man who had served the University for half a century died. Judge Richard C. Stoll had resigned from the Executive Committee in May, 1948, because of failing health, and Guy Huguelet had been elected chairman in his place. Stoll continued as a member of the board until his death. Appointed in 1898 when he was only twenty-two years of age, he served until 1949 with the exception of the years 1904 to 1907.

Since the Kentucky Court of Appeals in 1942 had decided that University personnel were subject to the $5,000

4 Minutes of Executive Committee, August 23, 1946, May 22, 1947, May 24, 1948; McVey Diary, February 19, 1947, October 19, 1948; Lexington Herald-Leader, April 6, August 17, 1947; Louisville Courier-Journal, December 11, 1946, December 17, 1947; Kentucky Kernel, August 2, 1946, June 27, 1947; Lexington Herald, December 4, 1945, September 23, October 23, 1946, January 28, 1947, November 8, 1948, October 30, 1949; Lexington Leader, December 3, 1947, February 24, December 1, 1948, November 29, 1949; L. S. Thompson to L. M. Chamberlain, July 15, 1949, Maurice Seay to Donovan, May 22, 1948, Donovan Papers; Thompson, "Books at the University of Kentucky," p. 65; Jacqueline Bull, "The Samuel M. Wilson Library," Register of the Kentucky Historical Society, XLVII (1949), 52-54; Minutes of Board of Trustees, July 19, 1946, September 25, December 18, 1948.

salary limitation set in Kentucky's constitution, some salaries had been supplemented from restricted funds given to the University. As inflation became more serious, it became obvious that other means must be found to pay the higher salaries necessary to retain the University's staff. There seemed a possibility that the constitution might be revised in 1947, but the conservative elements in the state defeated the issue at the polls. Anticipating defeat of the constitutional issue, the University had already moved in another direction. It had raised the salary of Louis Pardue, professor of physics, to $5,600, and a suit had been filed to test the University's right to do this. Judge Charles I. Dawson of Louisville took the case for the University and argued it before the Court of Appeals in October, 1947. In November, shortly after the issue of a constitutional convention had been defeated, the court handed down a decision which reversed the one made back in 1942. Once again presidents and professors at the University and the teachers colleges were held to be employees and not state officials, and thus not subject to the salary limitation. In 1949, however, an amendment to the state constitution finally raised the salary limitation to $12,000. The question of whether or not this new limitation applied to the University personnel would still be a matter for the courts to decide.[5]

Near the end of the McVey administration the American Chemical Society had begun to function as an accrediting agency. In 1940 a committee had visited Kentucky's Chemistry Department and refused to approve it. The society was especially critical of the heavy teaching loads carried by members of the department, the low salaries, the small amount of time which chemistry majors could

[5] Minutes of Board of Trustees, December 10, 1946, June 3, December 16, 1947, September 20, 1949; Donovan to Stoll, May 25, 1948, Donovan Papers; Donovan, *Keeping the University Free and Growing*, pp. 24-27; Minutes of Executive Committee, May 22, October 21, 1947.

give to courses in the humanities, and the fact that the number of staff members of the department holding the Ph.D. degree had dropped to four. Another member of the society criticized the practice of using full-time members of the staff to perform what he described as menial tasks and clerical duties.

In a move to correct this situation Donovan, shortly after becoming President, asked persons who had graduated in chemistry at Kentucky to tell him what they thought was wrong with the department. This brought a flood of letters from chemists all over the country. Their suggestions covered about the same ground as had been covered by the American Chemical Society, although some believed that the difficulties centered around the personality of the department head.

When Dr. Laurence L. Quill was brought to Kentucky as the new head of the Department of Chemistry, he made great strides toward meeting the requirements of the American Chemical Society, but he stayed only a year and a half. His successor, Dr. Lyle R. Dawson, continued the efforts to improve the department, and in 1946 it gained full recognition. In 1949 another inspection was made and recognition was continued. The chief need now, as the society pointed out, was a more adequate building.[6]

[6] Robert E. Swain to R. N. Maxson, March 5, 1940, Swain to McVey, March 5, 30, 1940, McVey to Swain, March 19, 22, 1940, Maxson to Thomas P. Cooper, December 16, 1940, April 28, 1941, Cooper to Maxson, December 18, 1940, Cooper to Erle M. Billings, May 13, 1941, Billings to Cooper, May 15, 1941, University of Kentucky Archives; B. S. Hopkins to Paul Boyd, December 11, 1941, Donovan to Guy B. Taylor, December 11, 1941, Maxson to Billings, March 9, 1942, Maxson to Donovan, March 12, May 11, 1942, Donovan to Maxson, May 11, 1942, Billings to Laurence L. Quill, September 15, 1943, April 17, 1944, Billings to Donovan, September 15, 1943, April 26, 1946, Donovan to Billings, September 18, 1943, Quill to Donovan, April 1, 1944, Quill to Billings, December 19, 1944, Lyle R. Dawson to Billings, November 2, 1945, Dawson to Donovan, November 13, 1945, February 15, 1946, Billings to Dawson, July 25, 1949, Donovan Papers. Letters from alumni who graduated in chemistry, all read but too numerous to list, may be seen in the Donovan Papers.

Like McVey, Donovan devoted a part of his time to public relations. Their methods, however, were quite different. McVey's was indirect. When asked to make a talk, he would choose a subject in the field of economics or foreign relations and hope that his audience would see the University behind what he was saying. Donovan presented the University directly to the people of the state. He coined two slogans which he used frequently: "The State of Kentucky is the Campus of the University," and "You cannot have a great state without a great state university."

Following the war, Donovan became convinced that the University of Kentucky would never receive proper financial support until it satisfied the desire of a highly vocal portion of the population for a good football team. At a meeting in November, 1945, the Executive Committee approved articles of incorporation for the University of Kentucky Athletic Association. It also approved an agreement between the University and the Athletic Association under which the association was given the use of Stoll Field and of the Alumni Gymnasium. The board of directors of the association would consist of the President of the University and ten other members, five of whom must be members of the faculty, one an alumnus, one a member of the Board of Trustees, and one the president of the Student Government Association. The Executive Committee believed that under this management no outside group could ever gain control of the University's athletic program.

In December of this year, 1945, Donovan called a meeting of thirty-six Lexington citizens who were known to be interested in football and told them that the University was ready to launch a major athletic program, but that it would not do so until $100,000 had been raised and placed in the bank against a possible "rainy day." This group raised $113,000, and deposited it to the credit of the Athletic Association. After his retirement Donovan wrote that the tale of the University Athletic Association was a great success story. "It has paid all the expenses of a splendid athletic program. The sports-loving public has relieved the taxpayers of this burden by picking up the check for this activity of the University."

Under the new organization, Bernie Shively, who had proved his ability as an athletic director, was retained in that position. Paul Bryant, a graduate of the University of Alabama and at the time head football coach at the University of Maryland, was brought to Kentucky to produce a winning team. In 1946 Kentucky played a ten-game schedule, winning seven and losing three, and football made money for the first time in the school's history. In 1947 the record was eight wins and three losses. One of the victories was over Villanova in the postseason Great Lakes Bowl at Cleveland. The 1948 season was less successful than the preceding one. Five games were won, three were lost and two were tied. In 1949 eleven games were played in the regular season. Eight were won and three lost. In the Orange Bowl at Miami on January 2, 1950, Santa Clara defeated Kentucky by a score of 21 to 13.

Basketball, already a successful sport at Kentucky, went on to new heights. The Southeastern Conference Tournament was won each season from 1945 to 1950, and the teams participated in at least one other postseason tournament each year, winning the National Invitational Tournament in 1946 and the National Collegiate Athletic Association Tournament in 1948, 1949, and 1951. The high mark was the 1947-1948 season, when Kentucky, the NCAA champion, entered the Olympic Trials Tournament, then played pre-Olympic exhibition games during the summer, and finally formed part of the United States team which won a gold medal at the Olympic Games in London.[7]

7 Donovan, *Keeping the University Free and Growing*, pp. 104-12, 138; Minutes of Executive Committee, November 24, 1945; *Kentucky Kernel*, November 30, 1945, January 18, 1946.

The acquisition by the University of the Louisville College of Pharmacy was a move that Donovan came to see also as a valuable one in the University's relations with the rest of the state. Two years before Donovan took office, the owners of the Louisville school had proposed a merger with the University, a proposal which was turned down at the time. In 1947 the idea was revived. Donovan was quite favorable to this acquisition because he believed that it offered a type of training which the University should be providing. The pharmacy school deeded its property in Louisville to the University, and on July 1, 1947, it became the institution's seventh college, Dr. Earl J. Slone continuing as dean. The College of Pharmacy would remain in Louisville until facilities could be provided on the Lexington campus.

As Donovan came to see it, the drugstore had replaced the general store as a gathering place in the average Kentucky town, and the pharmacists who operated them would now have an interest in the University. It was likely, he felt, that they would transmit some of their feeling to people who gathered in their stores, many of whom had previously given little thought to the University.[8]

The idea of a system of junior colleges scattered over the state, but operated by the University, had been suggested as early as 1930. Community leaders of the town of Paintsville in eastern Kentucky proposed that the property of their defunct Mayo College be turned over to the University. There was immediate opposition from both private and state colleges, because they anticipated eventual competition for students. In 1932 a similar proposal was made at Paducah in western Kentucky, and by 1934

[8] Minutes of Board of Trustees, September 19, December 15, 1939, February 25, March 11, April 1, December 16, 1947, June 25, 1948; Lexington *Leader,* March 26, 1947; Donovan, *Keeping the University Free and Growing,* pp. 46-47, 66; Minutes of Executive Committee, October 19, 1939, July 18, 1947.

the people of Ashland were talking of establishing a junior college. The University's thought had been, at first, that junior colleges should be under the control of the educational systems in the communities where they were established, but in 1948 the University did agree to establish one off-campus center on an experimental basis in the Covington-Newport area in northern Kentucky. In that populous area a great many high school graduates did not go on to college.

In February, 1948, the Board of Trustees approved the establishment of the Northern Extension Center, which would begin operation in the fall of that year. The center would be administered by the Department of University Extension, but no teachers could be employed without the approval of the heads of the various departments on the University campus. William C. Wesley, head of the Department of Education at Baldwin-Wallace College, was named director. Wesley resigned at the end of the center's first year and was succeeded by Thomas L. Hankins, for five years head of the Department of Industrial Education at the University.

Students could earn two years of residence credit at the center, in a limited number of fields. Also a few upper division and graduate courses were offered by extension. The Northern Extension Center, however, had a misleading name, which gave the impression that all credit earned there was extension credit. Actually this was true only of credit earned beyond the first two years of work, but misunderstandings sometimes resulted when students sought to transfer to other colleges or universities.

The center filled an important need in that it enabled many students who could not have left home in order to go to college to live at home and do so. Those who have been able to continue their last two years of study on the Lexington campus have done work in every way equal to that done by students who came to the campus as freshmen.[9]

In 1904 the Kentucky General Assembly had passed the Day Act forbidding the teaching of white and Negro students in mixed classes, an act aimed at Berea College, the only school in the state then engaged in the practice. But the law could be applied to other schools in the state as well. Under the Day Act, Negro teachers were severely handicapped as requirements for Kentucky teachers were raised. Except for those who were near enough to attend the Kentucky State College for Negroes at Frankfort, these people had to go out of the state to earn the credits they were required to have. White teachers, on the other hand, could take extension courses offered by the University in any town where there was sufficient demand. In September, 1931, the Board of Trustees of the University moved to relieve the situation by approving a plan under which extension classes for Negroes would be given on the same basis as for whites. To avoid any possible violation of the Day Law, even their grades were segregated. They were recorded, not in the office of the registrar of the University of Kentucky, but at the Kentucky State College for Negroes at Frankfort.

The first Negro to attempt to enter the University was Charles L. Eubanks, who applied for admission in 1941 to study civil engineering, which was not offered at the Negro school in Frankfort. Because of the Day Law, Registrar Leo M. Chamberlain refused to admit him.

[9] Lexington *Leader,* March 16, 1948; Louisville *Courier-Journal,* August 25, 1948; McVey Diary, January 25, February 25, March 1, 5, 6, 1930, March 31, 1932, June 21, 1934, January 17, March 20, 1935, January 11, November 4, December 31, 1937, March 17, 1938; Minutes of University Senate, November 12, 1934; Minutes of University Faculty, August 11, 1948; Minutes of Board of Trustees, February 14, 1946; Minutes of Executive Committee, March 16, 1948, July 15, 1949; William C. Wesley to Louis Clifton, May 28, 1949, Donovan Papers; *Kentucky Kernel,* July 9, 1948.

Eubanks brought suit for admission, first in Fayette Circuit Court and then in the Federal District Court. Time after time the case was continued to the next term of court, because one side or the other was not ready or was planning some new tactic. Finally in 1945 it was dismissed by Federal Judge H. Church Ford for want of prosecution. Leave was granted to the plaintiff to reinstate the suit, but this was never done.[10]

In 1948, John Wesley Hatch, a Negro, applied for admission to the College of Law. Instead, he was admitted to Kentucky State College with the understanding that the University would provide for his instruction. For a time law professors drove from Lexington to Frankfort to teach him, and he was given the privilege of using the State Law Library. In November, 1948, four Frankfort lawyers were employed to continue his instruction. Hatch's chief objection to the plan was that he had no opportunity to talk about his courses with fellow students. At the end of one semester he withdrew, and this experiment came to an end.

Also in 1948, Lyman T. Johnson, a Negro who taught in the Louisville school system and who held a master's degree from the University of Michigan, had applied for admission to the graduate school and had been refused. Johnson brought suit in Federal District Court and won his case. Judge Ford ordered the University to admit Negroes to its Graduate School and to its Colleges of Law,

10 *Kentucky Kernel,* October 21, 1941, May 14, July 9, 1943, January 14, 1944; Prentice Thomas to Leo M. Chamberlain, September 13, 1941, Donovan to Stoll, September 19, 1941, Graham to Donovan, September 26, 1941, Donovan to John W. Brooker, September 29, 1941, Samuel M. Wilson to Donovan, January 16, 1943, January 22, 1945, Donovan Papers; Minutes of Board of Trustees, September 16, 22, 1941; McVey, *The Gates Open Slowly,* pp. 153-59; McVey Diary, January 19, 21, 23, February 3, 15, 17, March 11, April 23, 1939, September 20, October 4, 1941, July 10, 1943; Minutes of Executive Committee, November 22, 1941, March 1, 1944: Donovan, *Keeping the University Free and Growing,* pp. 95-101.

Engineering, and Pharmacy, comparable work not being available at Frankfort.

At the next meeting of the board, Donovan presented the issue and recommended that the decision be accepted without appeal to a higher court. After a heated discussion, the board voted 7 to 5 in favor of appealing the case. It was the first time that one of Donovan's recommendations had been turned down by the board. The discussion, however, did not end with the taking of the vote. At this time Judge Stoll, who had less than three months to live, took charge of the situation. He stated that he had voted against Donovan's recommendation, but would like to reconsider. He also reminded the other members that when the board followed the recommendation of the President, it seldom made a mistake. Another vote was taken, and it stood ten to two against appeal and in favor of the admission of Negroes. In the summer of 1949 Johnson and twenty-nine others registered and attended the sessions without incident. Donovan's position and the University's handling of the situation received much favorable comment.[11]

Donovan's use of the new Athletic Association to make a new day in the University's football experience illustrates an interesting factor in this administration. Here was a President who made decisions slowly and cautiously, but who recognized the value of other men's ideas. In time he saw the worth of a University center out in the state. Upon later thought he recognized the closeness of a pharmacist in a small-town drugstore to people who should be told more about the work of the University. He wrote to old students to find out the weaknesses of the chemistry

[11] Donovan, *Keeping the University Free and Growing*, pp. 95-101; McVey Diary, November 5, 1948; *Kentucky Kernel*, March 26, June 25, November 19, 1948, April 1, 1949; Minutes of Board of Trustees, May 3, June 25, August 9, December 18, 1948.

work at the University. He risked promising young men like Elvis Stahr and Frank Dickey in important places. He put faith in his subordinates, men like Dean A. D. Kirwan who took the responsibility for and skillfully dealt with such problems as the touchy matter of veterans' housing. The breadth of his view is shown in the slogan for the University which he drew from out of his experience, "The State of Kentucky is the Campus of the University."

CHAPTER XIV

COMPLETING THE PATTERN

PRESIDENT DONOVAN, near the close of his administration, saw the University move to the fulfillment of the ideal pattern of a university with liberal arts, professional, and graduate divisions. After many years the legislature finally appropriated the money for the establishment of a medical center to include the professional colleges of medicine, dentistry, and nursing. In contrast to this auspicious move was the involvement of the University in the basketball scandals which came to light in the early fifties. Except for this interruption, however, the University moved forward quietly during Donovan's final years in office. Some new buildings were added to the campus, the staff grew in size, and enrollment climbed slowly after a slight decrease at the beginning of the decade. When Donovan handed over the administration of the University to his successor, one might truly say that the pattern laid out in the preceding century by James K. Patterson was essentially complete.

When, in October, 1951, three members of the 1948-1949 basketball team were arrested on a charge of accepting bribes to control the point spread in a National Invitational Tournament game between Kentucky and Loyola, the University was profoundly shocked. Some forewarning might have come when earlier several athletes from other colleges had been charged with the same offense, but Coach Adolph Rupp had stated with assurance: "The gamblers couldn't touch our boys with a ten-foot pole!" As the investigation proceeded, other instances of bribery were found, and three members of the 1949-1950 team were accused. Of the six, five pleaded guilty and were given suspended sentences. The sixth pleaded not guilty and was tried, but not convicted. The case against him was finally dismissed. In handing out the suspended sentences, Judge Saul Streit of New York issued a lengthy condemnation of the University and its athletic and even academic practices. He charged that the trustees and alumni had an "inordinate desire" for a profitable top-ranking sports program and that the University and athletic officials had winked at various abuses.

These charges were answered in a statement prepared at a joint meeting of the Executive Committee of the Board of Trustees, the board of directors of the Athletic Association, and the executive committee of the Alumni Association. The Athletic Association, the statement pointed out, was a nonprofit organization whose income was used to support the entire athletic program as well as other educational and cultural purposes. Nor was the desire for winning teams, the statement continued, peculiar to the alumni of the University of Kentucky. While the administration and the athletic staffs assumed part of the responsibility for what had happened, ultimate responsibility must be shared by the public which supported gambling, by overeager alumni, and by other university administrative officials and coaches.

Following the investigations in New York, the Southeastern Conference looked into the situation at the invitation of the University. Finding violations of conference rules, officials ruled that Kentucky could not play any Southeastern Conference teams during the 1952-1953 season. While the University was in the process of scheduling other games, the National Collegiate Athletic Association banned all University basketball games for the season. The penalty against the University amounted to a fine of approximately $100,000, which was about the annual income from basketball, a severer penalty than that meted any other school involved. The penalty did not punish the guilty players, but the school and particularly the players on the 1952-1953 team who were not involved in any way. It was thought by many that the University had been made a scapegoat for an overemphasis upon athletics which was prevalent throughout most of the nation.[1]

For those who cried out for victories, there were plenty —not only in basketball but now in football. The 1950 season with ten wins and one loss brought to Kentucky its first Southeastern football championship, but the climax was the upset of Oklahoma in the Sugar Bowl. The next year Kentucky defeated Texas Christian in the Cotton Bowl. In 1953 Paul Bryant resigned to become head coach at Texas A. and M., and he was succeeded by Blanton Collier, assistant coach of the professional Cleveland Browns who had coached high school sports in Paris, Kentucky, for sixteen years. Collier's teams continued to have winning seasons through the remainder of the Donovan administration. Basketball jumped back into the limelight after the one-year suspension with a 25-0 record in 1953-1954, and the SEC championship was won that season and the next.

The teaching staff at the University of Kentucky had nearly doubled in size in the forties. In the academic year 1939-1940 the College of Arts and Sciences had 167 full-

[1] Donovan, *Keeping the University Free and Growing*, 112-16; McVey Diary, October 20, 30, December 2, 15, 1951, February 17, 28, May 2, 4, 9, 17, June 15, July 30, August 12, November 3, 16, 1952; *Kentucky Kernel*, October 26, 1951, February 22, November 7, 21, 1952; A. D. Kirwan to Donovan, January 25, 1952, Donovan to J. D. Williams, March 7, 1952, L. M. Chamberlain to Donovan, August 6, 1952, N. W. Dougherty to Donovan, August 18, 1952, Donovan Papers; William Clayton Bower to Judge Saul Streit, June 30, 1952, General File, 41-56, University of Kentucky Archives; Minutes of Board of Trustees, December 18, 1951; Answer to Judge Saul Streit, 5 pp. typescript in Donovan Papers; Donovan's appeal to Southeastern Conference, 6 pp. typescript in Donovan Papers; Copy of Decision of Southeastern Conference, 1 p. typescript in Donovan Papers.

time faculty members, and ten years later had over twice that number. In the same period the number of teachers in the College of Agriculture and Home Economics increased from forty-eight to seventy. In Engineering the increase was from thirty-eight to fifty-eight, in Law from eight to fifteen, and in Commerce from seventeen to thirty-six. In Education, however, the number remained almost constant, increasing only from sixty-two to sixty-four. At the same time the academic training of the staff also markedly increased with the number of doctorates rising from 113 to 216 and of master's degrees from 211 to 361.

Several changes in departmental organization were made in the early years of the 1950s. The Departments of Sociology and Rural Sociology were combined, with Dr. Howard Beers as chairman, since the previous head of the Sociology Department preferred to give his time to teaching, research, and writing. The Departments of German and Romance Languages were combined into a Department of Modern Foreign Languages, with Dr. Adolph E. Bigge as head. In the College of Agriculture the Departments of Farm Economics and of Markets and Rural Finance were combined to form a Department of Agricultural Economics, with Dr. Aubrey J. Brown as head. A Department of Air Science and Tactics was created, and the Department of Journalism became the School of Journalism. The name of the Department of English Language and Literature was changed to Department of English, Speech, and Dramatic Arts. Short courses in police work had been offered for several years, but in 1951 the University for the first time offered a Bachelor of Arts degree with a major in police administration.

Not all teaching at the University was done in regular classes. Much was accomplished in short courses, conventions, and special lectures. When Dr. Herman Spivey became head of the English Department, he began to bring outstanding literary figures to the campus for lectures both to students and to the public. When Spivey succeeded Dr. Louis Pardue, who had resigned in 1950 to become vice president of Virginia Polytechnic Institute, as Dean of the Graduate School, Dr. William S. Ward, who took over the English Department, continued these lectures. The History Department also brought from four to six of the best men in the field each year for the Blazer Lecture Series, made possible through the generosity of Paul Blazer, chairman of the board of the Ashland Oil and Refining Company, and his wife, Georgia Blazer, who was a member of the University Board of Trustees.[2]

More and more the faculty of the University were participating in educational work at other institutions and in foreign countries. Members of the staff taught at nearly all the ranking universities of the country, among them Johns Hopkins, California, Harvard, Wisconsin, and the Massachusetts Institute of Technology. Many of the faculty also went abroad in various advisory capacities. Herman Spivey and Leo Chamberlain went to India for the State Department; Lawrence Thompson went to Trinidad in a survey of the East Caribbean Regional Library. Irwin Sanders visited the Balkans; Clement Eaton went to England, and Amry Vandenbosch and Morris Scherago to Southeast Asia. In 1956 the University entered into a long-term agreement to offer educational and scientific services to the University of Indonesia.[3]

[2] Minutes of Board of Trustees, May 30, 1950, June 1, 1951, April 25, June 3, September 16, 1952; *Kentucky Kernel,* January 13, June 23, 30, July 21, December 1, 1950, January 19, September 21, November 2, 1951, September 18, 1952; Minutes of Executive Committee, February 17, October 25, 1950, July 21, 1951.

[3] *Kentucky Kernel,* October 30, 1953, April 23, October 29, 1954, May 25, June 22, July 13, 1956; Lexington *Leader,* August 6, 1956; Minutes of Board of Trustees, April 7, June 2, 1953, June 22, 1956; Minutes of Executive Committee, May 16, October 16, 1953, July 16, 1954.

Several members of the staff during this period also held offices in national or regional organizations. Donovan was vice president of the National Association of State Universities in 1953-1954 and was president the next year; at the same time he served on the board of trustees of Peabody College. Dean Terrell of the College of Engineering was president of the American Society of Civil Engineers, while Thomas D. Clark held the same office in the Mississippi Valley Historical Association. Lyman Ginger held the office of vice president of the National Education Association.[4]

A number of administrative changes took place in the University during these six years. In 1950 Dean Maurice Seay resigned to accept a position at the University of Chicago, and the office of Dean of the University was abolished. With the departure of Seay, A. D. Kirwan's office of Dean of Men became Dean of Students, and the agencies concerned with student activities which had reported to Seay were now administered by Dean Kirwan. Kirwan, however, resigned his deanship in 1954 to devote all of his time to teaching and research, and the title of the office once more became Dean of Men. As the business affairs of the University became more complex, a new administrative arrangement was needed to handle them efficiently. In 1954 Frank Peterson assumed the new office of Vice President (Business Administration), and George Kavanaugh moved into Peterson's place as comptroller. In the same year Lyman Ginger became dean of the newly created College of Adult and Extension Education; this new position made him responsible for all extension

4 *Kentucky Kernel*, March 13, May 8, July 17, September 25, 1953, November 19, 1954, February 24, April 27, 1956; Minutes of Board of Trustees, January 11, April 5, 1955; Minutes of Executive Committee, May 22, 1954; Frank Welch to Donovan, May 20, 1953, Donovan to J. D. Williams, February 1, 1954, Williams to Donovan, May 7, 1955, Elmer Ellis to Donovan, May 22, 1955, Donovan Papers; Lexington *Herald*, November 10, 1953, June 25, September 8, 1955.

and correspondence courses, for evening classes, and for the Northern Center at Covington. Elvis Stahr, who had proved his ability as Dean of the College of Law and as an assistant to the Secretary of the Army, was given the additional title of provost, in which capacity he was to devote part of his time to soliciting funds for the University. The University Faculty was also changed slightly during these six years; in 1952 its representation was reapportioned and the size of the body was doubled.[5]

The faculty at the University was increasingly productive in research. As in the past, perhaps the most active of all departments was the Agricultural Experiment Station, which continued its work in improving the growth and processing of tobacco as well as in other areas of agriculture. It was estimated that the tobacco research alone had more than repaid all the money which the state had contributed to the support of the University since its founding. The work of the Experiment Station was expanded in 1955 with the acquisition of a 600-acre farm in Owen County; this farm would make possible a more scientific study of the problems peculiar to the Eden Shale region which extended into thirty-two of Kentucky's counties. Bacteriology, Engineering, and Chemistry were also engaged in active research programs, and in the Department of Sociology a Bureau of Community Service was created to study the problems of local communities and to suggest remedies.

The publication of faculty research was greatly encouraged by the University of Kentucky Press. In 1950 Bruce F. Denbo became the first full-time director of the Press, and the annual production markedly increased. A major project was undertaken by the University through the

[5] Minutes of Executive Committee, July 21, 1951, October 16, 1953; Donovan to J. S. Chambers, April 12, 1954, Donovan Papers; Louisville *Courier-Journal*, April 1, 1954, June 8, 1955; Minutes of Board of Trustees, April 6, 1954, April 5, 1955.

Press in 1952 with the decision to edit and publish the papers of Kentucky's greatest statesman, Henry Clay. Dr. James F. Hopkins of the History Department was selected as editor of this work. Kentucky thus joined other states and universities in making available the carefully edited papers of America's early leaders. During the early fifties the University was also the home of four scholarly journals, *The Journal of Farm Economics, The Journal of Southern History, The Kentucky Law Journal,* and *Rural Sociology.*

The growth of the University library kept pace with the faculty and its research. By 1956 the library's holdings totaled over 700,000 volumes; this placed it fourth among libraries of the southeastern United States. *Library Trends,* a journal published at the University of Illinois, ranked it first in quality in that region. Certain collections acquired during the early fifties heightened the quality; over 2,000 volumes were given from the estate of President Emeritus McVey, who died in 1953, a collection of the papers of Zachary Taylor were presented by J. Stephen Watkins, and important papers of Cassius M. Clay, who had been chairman of the convention which had drafted Kentucky's present constitution, were given by his son. In 1952 the Margaret I. King Library was accepted as a member of the Association of Research Libraries; at that time only forty-five other libraries in the United States and Canada qualified for membership.

Enrollment and income also steadily increased. By 1956 enrollment once more approached ten thousand, standing at 9,509 including 968 at the Northern Extension Center. For the biennium 1954-1956 the University's income was $22,065,158.85, to which the state contributed $9,545,930.07.

To handle the increasing activities of the school, other buildings were constructed.

In 1950 three of these were dedicated. The Fine Arts Building, housing the Departments of Art and Music and the Guignol Theater, was dedicated in February as a part of the Founders Week program. Memorial Coliseum had three dedications. On Memorial Day it was dedicated as an auditorium for public and university meetings, with Dr. Daniel E. Poling as the principal speaker. On the following October 25 it was dedicated for use as a concert hall just prior to a program by James Melton. Then on December 9, it was dedicated as a sports center, when the first basketball game was played on its floor with Kentucky defeating Purdue 70 to 52. The new Service Building on Limestone Street with two floors and a basement for the Department of Maintenance and Operations and one floor for library overflow was dedicated on December 8, 1950.

A new Journalism Building, located between McVey Hall and the Mining Laboratory and partially paid for by the Kernel Press and by bookstore profits, was dedicated on November 2, 1951, with Don Whitehead, former University of Kentucky student and Pulitzer Prize winning war correspondent, as the speaker. This building, named in honor of Professor Enoch Grehan, contained two floors and a basement in which the University printing plant found a new home. The removal of all printing equipment from the basement of McVey Hall provided space there for the University of Kentucky Press, which had been located in a former dwelling house.

By the end of 1952 an addition to the Agricultural Engineering Building had been started, and the first wing of a Mineral Industries Building on Graham Avenue had been completed. The latter provided quarters for the Department of Mines and Minerals and for the Kentucky Geological Survey.[6]

[6] Minutes of Executive Committee, February 17, 1950, July 21, 1951, May 17, July 18, 1952; *The University of Kentucky: Its History and*

More students necessitated more housing. Donovan Hall, a dormitory for men, was dedicated on May 30, 1955. Keeneland Hall, a dormitory for women, was located north of Patterson Hall and was dedicated on October 17 of the same year. The temporary buildings in Cooperstown were replaced by permanent apartment buildings, and plans were made to do the same in Shawneetown. Several smaller buildings were erected and leased to fraternities or sororities. With the exception of a $200,000 gift from the Keeneland Foundation, all of these buildings were financed by the sale of bonds which would be retired by income from rents. In 1956 another dormitory for women was started; it was to be called Holmes Hall.

In every institution, disagreements occur from time to time, and even the most skillful administrator cannot always resolve them to the pleasure of everyone. Two such problems came about during the last six years of Donovan's presidency. One of them, which involved the Department of Agronomy, was over the relative merits of grass known as Kentucky 31 fescue. The conflicting reports on the grass as pasturage puzzled the state's farmers, and when the head of the department retired in January, 1950, his successor was promoted from within the department with the understanding that the question would be resolved. The situation, however, got no better, and eventually it was decided that yet another department head should be appointed. This move brought charges from the successor to the former head that he had been demoted without a fair hearing. The case was investigated by the local chapter of the American Association of Uni-

Development, pp. 22, 31; McVey Diary, February 23, 25, May 30, September 17, 25, 26, October 25, December 9, 10, 1950, January 9, November 2, 1951; Louisville *Courier-Journal*, February 14, 1952; Lexington *Leader*, October 24, 1950; Minutes of Faculty, October 13, November 10, 1952; Minutes of Board of Trustees, May 30, September 19, December 12, 1950, June 1, December 18, 1951, September 16, December 19, 1952.

versity Professors which found that neither tenure nor academic freedom were involved.[7]

Another problem arose when the Fine Arts Building was opened to the public. At that time an exhibit was held of works by various members of the Art Department. The public apparently did not care for this exhibit, and President Donovan became worried for fear that the people would not support an art program which they did not understand. The department head defended the work of the department, pointing out that it was not greatly different from that of other departments in the South and that the teachers' personal creative work did not interfere with their teaching of traditional approaches in their classes. In March, 1951, an exhibit was held of representative works of the art faculties of ten state universities in the Southeast. The head of the University department thought the exhibit showed rather well what was being done in other departments and how Kentucky compared with them. At the end of the academic year 1950-1951, the department head offered his resignation whenever a suitable replacement could be found so that he might give full time to teaching and scholarship.[8]

A significant move was taken in education when the University decided to participate in a southern regional

[7] McVey Diary, January 5, 11, February 2C, 1950; *Kentucky Kernel*, December 16, 1949, February 24, October 20, 25, 1950, January 12, 1951; Donovan, *Keeping the University Free and Growing*, pp. 38-39; "The Story of Kentucky 31 Fescue," *Kentucky Farmer*, LXXXV (May, 1949), 4; Minutes of Board of Trustees, December 13, 1949, April 15, June 3, September 16, 1952; Weeks to Donovan, July 1, 1952, Donovan to Weeks, July 2, 1952, Donovan Papers; Louisville *Courier-Journal*, April 30, May 4, 28, 1952; Lexington *Leader*, April 28, 30, May 2, 17, 27, 1952; Lexington *Herald*, January 9, 1948, April 29, May 27, July 2, 3, 1952.

[8] McVey Diary, December 11, 14, 1949, September 18, 1951; Donovan's notes on conference with Chamberlain, White, and Rannells, January 25, 1950, Donovan Papers; Annual Report of Department of Art, 1949-50, Rannells' notes on conference with Donovan, Chamberlain, and White, January 25, 1950, "Review of Art Department Controversy," 3 pp. typescript, Art Department File, University of Kentucky Archives.

program in which the schools would pool their resources and eliminate wasteful and expensive duplication of work. The first plan to go into effect under this program was a cooperative arrangement between the University and Alabama Polytechnic Institute by which a limited number of University students after the satisfactory completion of two years preveterinary study could enter the Veterinary School at Auburn. Earlier the University, working with the University of Tennessee and the University of Alabama, had set up a cooperative program for study leading to the master's degree in public administration.

One of the most important accomplishments of the University during President Donovan's tenure of office was the establishment of the University's Medical Center. Early in the McVey administration there had been occasional mention of the need for a medical school at the University of Kentucky. The only medical school in the state was at the University of Louisville; however, it did not graduate enough physicians to supply Kentucky with an adequate number, and many of those who did graduate there went outside of the state to practice. In 1930 Dr. John S. Chambers, head of the Department of Hygiene and Public Health, told McVey that thirty of Kentucky's counties had an average of one doctor for 2,100 people, and that sixteen counties had only one for 3,100.

In the 1930 legislative session a bill was introduced in the House to provide for the establishment of a medical school in connection with Western Kentucky State Teachers College at Bowling Green. This brought immediate action from McVey. Through the newspapers he pointed out that if such a school were established, it should be located in Lexington and operated by the University of Kentucky. Bowling Green was located directly between the Vanderbilt and the Louisville Medical schools, it did not have hospital facilities comparable to those in Lexington, and Western was not equipped to offer the type of premedical training that was available at the University. The Bowling Green bill died in committee.

The first efforts by the University to secure a medical school of its own were hampered by the depression. In the fall of 1930, McVey, while attending a meeting in New York, discussed with some of the educational foundations the possibility of help in starting a College of Medicine. They were sympathetic, but none of the foundations were doing anything in the medical field at that time. Seven years later, Governor A. B. Chandler expressed interest in a medical school, but the depression had not ended and funds would have been hard to raise.

World War II had hardly ended before Dr. Chambers was at work again. He discussed the matter with McVey, with President Donovan, and with Dr. Fred Rankin, a leading member of the medical profession in Lexington. Dr. Rankin was favorable, but did not agree with Chambers that a large amount of money might be contributed by individuals. He believed that the University would have to depend upon the state, the federal government, and perhaps some of the foundations. Federal aid for a hospital might be obtained under the Hill-Burton Act which required the state to furnish only 29 percent of the total cost. Donovan was cautious about asking the legislature for an appropriation, because he feared that money allowed for a medical school might mean less for the other branches of the University.

At the same time the University of Louisville was seeking state aid for its medical school. Donovan pointed out that the Louisville institution had been held by the courts to be a private school and that its trustees and administration wanted it to be considered a private school so that it would not be subject to the salary limitations and purchasing regulations which plagued the state's public institutions. It seemed to him that if the University of Louisville Medical School could receive money from the legislature on the ground that it was rendering a valuable service to the state, the same argument might then be used to obtain state money for Louisville's College of Dentistry, its College of Law, its Speed Scientific School, or its School of Social Work. The result would be the establishment of a second state university even though Kentucky had never given adequate support to the one that it had. "To permit the Medical School of the University of Louisville to receive public assistance . . . would erase the line of demarcation between public and private institutions," he said. Kentucky's Attorney General, Eldon S. Dummit, however, advised the chairman of Louisville's Board of Trustees that state aid for a private institution was not permitted by Kentucky's constitution. The University of Kentucky Faculty passed a resolution to the effect that if the University of Louisville could not continue to operate its medical school, its ownership be transferred to the University of Kentucky.

When the legislature met in 1948, several bills dealing with medical education were introduced. Some of these provided for the establishment of a medical school at the University of Kentucky, but none of them passed. A bill did pass, however, appropriating $250,000 for medical research in the 1948-1950 biennium. Donovan urged Governor Earle Clements to veto any such bill, but the Governor did not do so. The *Courier-Journal* remarked that this legislation was designed to aid the University of Louisville. "It thus becomes the first institution not a member of the state school system to get state financial aid."

In the 1950 session of the legislature a bill to create a medical school at the University of Kentucky was introduced in the House, but again it failed to pass. A Senate resolution directing the Board of Trustees to study ways and means of providing more doctors for Kentucky's rural areas was introduced. Although it was signed by sixteen senators, it never came to a vote. The indirect $125,000 annual appropriation to the University of Louisville Medical School was continued for two more years.

In 1951, at the invitation of Dr. Sam Overstreet, president of the Kentucky State Medical Association, and Dr. Murray Kinsman, Dean of the University of Louisville Medical School, the American Medical Association's Council on Medical Education and Hospitals sent its secretary and its associate secretary to Kentucky. They held a two-day conference with Donovan, the mayor of Louisville, the acting President of the University of Louisville, the two doctors that had invited them, and other interested physicians. In their report these two specialists in medical education recommended that the state continue to make indirect grants to the University of Louisville, but that it also establish a medical school at the University of Kentucky.

In 1952 the Board of Trustees of the University issued a booklet on medical education in Kentucky, which was distributed to members of the legislature as well as to the newspapers and to many of the doctors of the state. The booklet contained some valuable information about the medical situation in Kentucky. The state had only one doctor for 1,140 persons, and the ratio was growing worse every year. The nation had one doctor for 740 persons. The seven states bordering Kentucky had seventeen medical schools, but these had admitted a total of only fifteen Kentucky students in the preceding year. These seven states had one medical school for 1,800,000 people, while Kentucky had only one for about 3,000,000 people. The booklet suggested that the Legislative Research Commission study the possibility of establishing a medical school at Lexington and report to the 1954 legislature. This suggestion was accepted, but at the same time the indirect support for the University of Louisville Medical School was increased to $425,000 for the 1952-1954 biennium.

The Legislative Research Commission was assisted in its work by an Advisory Committee on Medical Education, consisting of five doctors, and by the Committee on Medical Education of the University Faculty of which Dr. Chamberlain was chairman. The Fayette County Medical Society unanimously endorsed the creation of the proposed school, but doctors from some parts of the state, for reasons best known to themselves, were bitterly opposed. At its meeting in December, 1953, the Board of Trustees went on record as favoring the establishment of a medical school whenever sufficient appropriations were made.

Dr. Francis Massie, chairman of the Fayette County Medical Society's committee on medical education, and J. Stephen Watkins of Lexington were instrumental in the formation of a Kentucky Medical Sciences Development Foundation which worked to obtain both public appropriations and private gifts for a medical school. On June 1, 1954, the Board of Trustees officially established such a school, but for the time being it existed only on paper.

In the fall of 1955 both of the candidates for the governorship promised to support the founding of a new medical school. A. B. Chandler, the winning candidate, recommended to the 1956 legislature that the sum of $5,000,000 be appropriated for the starting of a medical center which would include a 500-bed hospital, and which would cost a total of about $28,000,000. The proposed measure was passed, and a site on Rose Street at the northwest corner of the Experiment Station Farm was chosen.

In May, 1956, Colleges of Dentistry and Nursing were established, and the position of Vice President in charge of the Medical Center was created. After a list of fifty-two possibilities had been screened, Dr. William R. Willard, Dean of the College of Medicine at Syracuse University, was selected as Vice President of the Medical Center and Dean of the College of Medicine. It was expected that the school, when in full operation, would graduate seventy-five physicians each year.[9]

On March 17, 1956, President Donovan reached the age of sixty-nine. Under the rules of the University he could have continued in the same position for another year, but he preferred not to do so. In April he notified both the Board of Trustees and the Faculty of his desire to accept change-of-work on September 1, 1956. At that time he would complete fifty years as a teacher and an administrator, the last fifteen at the University of Kentucky.

"The position of President of the University is a grueling task," he told the board. "It requires long hours of work each day, and only a strong man has the energy and drive to meet the strain. The president must be mentally alert; he must have the vision to plan and execute programs, the patience of Job, the vitality to keep traveling, meeting people, making speeches, writing articles, resisting pressures from many sources, and he must have the courage to fight for the University against all odds when nothing but a fight can maintain its integrity. He must have the sense and sensitivity to recognize and use good counsel when offered him. I realize that age is taking its toll and I no longer have the energy I once had. My

9 Lexington *Herald*, March 10, 1950; Lexington *Leader*, March 2, 1930, February 13, 1953; Louisville *Courier-Journal*, January 23, March 27, 1948, February 24, 1950, February 26, 29, 1952; *Kentucky Kernel*, January 14, 1954; McVey Diary, 1930-1952, *passim;* Minutes of Faculty, April 14, 1947, January 12, 1953; Minutes of Board of Trustees, December 18, 1951, December 15, 1953, June 1, 1954, April 3, May 28, 1956; Minutes of Executive Committee, July 20, 1956; Donovan, *Keeping the University Free and Growing*, 50-55. The Donovan Papers contain many letters pertaining to the founding of the Medical School.

loyalty and devotion to my Alma Mater will not permit me to coast along for another year; I have no desire to fade out."

The President made it clear that he did not wish to take part in the selection of his successor. Instead, he urged the appointment of a screening committee consisting of both board members and faculty members, which would eventually make a recommendation or recommendations to the board. Governor Chandler appointed to this committee three board members, Robert Hobson, Harper Gatton, and Dr. Ralph Angelucci. From a list of ten nominated by the faculty he appointed Dr. H. Bruce Price, Robert E. Shaver, and John Kuiper.

After evaluating fifty-six presidential possibilities, this committee made its report to the Board of Trustees on June 22, 1956. It recommended four possibilities: Dr. Frank G. Dickey, Dean of the College of Education, Dr. Frank J. Welch, Dean of the College of Agriculture, Elvis Stahr, Provost and Dean of the College of Law, and Dr. Louis Pardue, Vice President of Virginia Polytechnic Institute and former Dean of the Graduate School at Kentucky. From this group the board at the same meeting named Dr. Dickey as the next President of the University. Dr. Dickey had received his A.B. at Transylvania College, with a major in English, his M.A. in English at Kentucky, and the degree of Ed.D. also at Kentucky. After becoming dean, he had completed a year of postdoctoral work at Harvard.

When President Donovan reviewed the accomplishments of his administration, he was especially pleased with the more friendly attitude which the public exhibited toward the University. "People in all parts of the state," he said in a letter to board member Harper Gatton, "now refer to the University as 'our University' instead of 'the University.'" One hundred and ten local alumni clubs had been started in the state and at least fifteen in large cities outside of the state.

In a period of forty-six years the University of Kentucky had been guided by three Presidents, Henry S. Barker, Frank L. McVey, and Herman L. Donovan. Barker had lacked the training and experience to be a successful administrator in the field of higher education. McVey had possessed both of these essentials, but he was handicapped by a lack of enough money to do the things that he had hoped to do. Donovan had been President at a time when more money was available. He had striven to obtain for the University the support that it needed. In this he had not been completely successful, but the money that the institution did receive he had used wisely.

The historian of the Patterson administration concluded that: "Patterson and those who worked with him had built well, and when the state should decide to create a great university, it had a solid foundation on which to build." McVey and Donovan had added several stories to the foundation which Patterson had laid. McVey's dream of membership in the Association of American Universities had been attained by only fifteen state universities when Donovan's administration came to an end, and Kentucky was not yet one of these. But the past was only the prologue, and many signs indicated that a greater future lay ahead.[10]

Under Frank G. Dickey the University enjoyed a period of great physical growth. The largest addition to the plant

10 Donovan to Governor Chandler and Members of the Board, April 3, 1956, Donovan Papers; Minutes of Faculty, April 9, May 14, 1956; Minutes of Board of Trustees, April 3, June 22, 1956; *Kentucky Kernel*, April 20, June 29, 1956; Lexington *Leader*, June 20, 1956; Donovan to Gatton, May 18, 1954, Donovan Papers; James F. Hopkins, *The University of Kentucky: Origins and Early Years* (Lexington, 1951), p. 294; *Journal of Proceedings and Addresses of the Fifty-sixth Annual Conference of the Association of American Universities and Seventh Annual Conference of the Association of Graduate Schools* (1955), pp. 156-60.

was the Albert B. Chandler Medical Center, built to house the Colleges of Medicine, Dentistry, and Nursing, and the University Hospital. Other structures completed were Holmes Hall and Blazer Hall, dormitories for women, Haggin Hall for men, a Physics-Chemistry Building, and a Pharmacy Building. New buildings were constructed for the off-campus centers at Covington, Henderson, and Cumberland. Additions to the library and the Student Union were completed. An Agricultural Science Center, an Alumni Building, and a new building for the College of Commerce were started.

John W. Oswald, scientist and former Vice President of the University of California became President of the University of Kentucky on September 1, 1963. During the two months that had elapsed since the end of the Dickey term the school had been capably administered by its Executive Vice President, Dr. A. D. Albright.

As the University looked toward the celebration of its first hundred years, Dr. Oswald, a man of boundless energy and sound ideas, was proving himself to be the leader that the University of Kentucky needed to meet the challenges of the future when the demands made upon it, upon the wisdom of its President, upon the knowledge of its faculty, and upon the people who support it, will be greater than ever before. But to meet the challenges the University has been prepared well by the work of the past Presidents and faculty and by the guidance of its trustees.

INDEX

Academy, 2, 5
Adams, Jesse E., 70, 146
Administration Building, 3-4, 54,
    59, 77, 90, 110, 120, 127
Adult and Extension Education,
    College of, 183-84
Adult education, 138
Aeronautical Research Laboratory,
    140
Agricultural Adjustment
    Administration, 107
Agricultural and Mechanical College
    of Kentucky, 1, 148, 162
Agricultural Building, 3, 55, 86, 118
Agricultural Economics,
    Department of, 181
Agricultural education, 69
Agricultural Education,
    Department of, 33
Agricultural Engineering Building,
    85, 186
Agricultural Experiment Station, 1,
    3-4, 6, 24-26, 33, 36, 42, 54-56, 74,
    105-107, 116-17, 140, 142, 184
Agricultural Experiment Station
    Farm, 78, 85, 161, 193
Agricultural Experiment
    Substations, 62, 78
Agricultural Extension, 54-55, 74,
    92, 106-107
Agricultural Extension, Department
    of, 32, 35-36, 54-55
Agricultural Extension, School of, 6
Agricultural Extension Service, 42
Agricultural Hall, 3, 55, 86, 118
Agricultural Science Center, 197
Agriculture, College of, 1, 4, 6, 8,
    24, 35-36, 42, 51-53, 55-56, 73, 85,
    106-107, 120, 132, 150, 165, 181,
    195
Agriculture, School of, 6
Agriculture and Home Economics,
    College of, 140, 181
Agriculture Building, 3, 55, 86, 118
Agronomy, Department of, 6, 187

Air Science and Tactics,
    Department of, 181
Albright, A. D., 197
Algernon Sidney Sullivan
    Medallion, 131
Allen, William R., 52
Alpha Delta Sigma, 14
Alpha Zeta, 14
Alumni Association 77, 179
Alumni Building, 197
Alumni Gymnasium, 77, 87
American Association of Colleges
    for Teacher Education, 154, 156
American Association of University
    Professors, 56, 154, 187-88
American Chemical Society, 168-69
American Institute of Electrical
    Engineers, 14
American Medical Association, 192
American Society of Mechanical
    Engineers, 14
Anatomy and Physiology, Depart-
    ment of, 6, 88, 111-12, 118, 132
Ancient Languages, Department of,
    103
Anderson, F. Paul, 1, 5, 12, 26, 28,
    37, 41, 44-45, 61, 95, 103, 164
Anderson, Walter S., 106, 132
Angelucci, Ralph, 195
Animal Husbandry, Department of,
    6
Animal Pathology Building, 146,
    162
Anthropology and Archeology,
    Department of, 72
Anthropology and Archeology,
    Museum of, 89-90, 127
Armory, 3, 15, 118
Army Specialized Training
    Program, 141
Art, Department of, 76, 88, 118,
    186, 188
Art and Design, Department of, 53,
    58
Arts, School of, 6

Arts and Science, College of, 1, 5-6, 11

Arts and Sciences, College of, 53, 72, 75, 95-96, 111, 129, 138, 150, 164-66, 180-81

Arts and Sciences lectures, 138

Ashland Oil and Refining Company, 182

Association of American Universities, 100, 196

Association of Land Grant Colleges and Universities, 106-107

Athletic Association, 62, 98, 163, 170-71, 176, 179

Athletic Council, 62, 77, 98-99

Athletics, Advisory Council on, 129-30

Athletics, Department of, 129

Athletics, Director of, 62, 129

Babcock, K. C., 57

Bacteriology, Department of, 6, 53, 58, 118, 120, 184

Bankhead-Jones Act, 109

Baptist State Board of Missions, 67

Barkenbus, Charles, 52, 132

Barker, Henry S., 1, 4-14, 18-22, 24-26, 29-31, 34-40, 43, 45-46, 53-54, 63, 196; defends academic freedom, 25-26; retirement recommended, 40; death of, 88

Barker Hall, 87

Baseball, 11-12

Basketball, 12-13, 79-80, 100, 114, 150, 171, 178-80

Beaumont, Henry, 96

Beers, Howard, 181

Berea College, 174

Best, Harry, 52

"Between-us Day," 50

Bigge, Adolph E., 132, 181

Biological Sciences, Division of, 138

Biological sciences, need for better housing, 86

Biological Sciences Building, 118, 164

Blanding, Sarah G., 108, 139; named as Dean of Women, 72

Blazer, Georgia, 182

Blazer, Paul, 182

Blazer Hall, 197

Blazer Lecture Series, 182

Board of Trustees, 2, 5-10, 14, 23, 29-31, 36-37, 39, 45, 48, 50, 52-53, 60-61, 68, 70-72, 76-78, 83, 85, 88, 94, 101, 103, 113, 115, 127, 129-30, 133-36, 140, 142-44, 153-55, 174, 179, 191-95; enlarged, 37; Rules and Regulations of, 59; reduced in size, 60

Boles, S. A., 114

Botany, Department of, 53, 58, 120, 127, 139, 162

Bowman, John B., 162

Bowman Hall, 162

Boyd, Paul P., 5, 46, 66

Boyd Hall, 76, 118

Bradley, William O., 85

Bradley Hall, 162

Brauer, Richard, 102

Breathitt County, 78

Breckinridge, W. C. P., 85

Breckinridge Hall, 162

Brown, Aubrey J., 181

Bryan, William Jennings, 16, 67-68

Bryant, Paul, 171, 180

Buell Armory, 3, 15, 118

Buildings and Grounds, Department of, 127, 134

Bureau, Ernest A., 52

Bureau of Business Research, 73, 88

Bureau of Community Service, 184

Bureau of Educational Service, 70, 73, 126, 142

Bureau of Engineering Research and Development, 142

Bureau of School Service, 70, 73, 126, 142

Business Management and Control, Department of, 134

Buttrick, Wallace, 30

Caldwell County, 78

Campus Book Store, 82, 135

Canterbury Club, 15

Capper-Ketcham Act, 92

Carnegie, Andrew, 4

Carpenter, Cecil C., 102, 164

Central Heating Plant, 117

Centre College, 89-90, 99

Chalkley, Lyman, 13, 29
Chamberlain, Leo M., 88, 133, 174, 182, 193; becomes Dean of University, 138; becomes Vice President, 165
Chambers, John S., 89, 189-90
Chandler, A. B., 110, 190, 193, 195
"Change of work" plan, 88-89
Chapman, Virgil, 16
Cheek, Frank J., 102
Chemistry, Department of, 71, 120, 132, 168-69, 184
Chemistry, School of, 3, 6-7
Chemistry Building, 3-4
Civil Engineering, College of, 1, 5, 16, 27, 37
Civil Engineering, Department of, 120, 164-65
Civil Engineering and Physics Building, 4, 120
Civil Works Administration, 105, 108
Clark, Champ, 16
Clark, Thomas D., 87, 89, 165-66, 183
Clay, Cassius M., 185
Clay, Henry, 184-85
Clements, Earle, 153, 191
Clifton Pond, 20
Clyde, Paul H., 87, 107
Coal Research Laboratory, 146
Coleman, J. Winston, 89
Collier, Blanton, 180
Colvin, George, 67-69
Commerce, College of, 73, 120, 123, 132, 150, 164-65, 181, 197; established, 70; need for better housing, 86
Commissioner of Agriculture, 25, 37, 60
Committee of Fifteen, 146-47
Committee on the State of the University, 124-25
Comptroller, position of created, 134-35
Cooper, Thomas P., 65, 88, 95, 106, 133-34, 146, 156; named as Dean of College of Agriculture and Director of Agricultural Extension, 51-52; President of Association of Southern Agricultural Workers,

Cooper, T. P. (*continued*):
56; Secretary-Treasurer of Association of Land Grant Colleges and Universities, 107; acting President, 131; retirement of, 155-56
Cooperstown, 161, 187
Cornell, C. B., 61, 65
Council on Public Higher Education, 92, 111, 128
Croft, Lysle W., 103
Crouse, Charles S., 52

Dairy Center, 162
Dairy Products Building, 85
Daniels, Lloyd C., 7
Dantzler, L. L., 132
Davis, J. Morton, 46, 101
Dawson, Charles I., 168
Dawson, Lyle R., 169
Day Act, 174
Dean of Men, 135
Dean of Students, position created, 183
Dean of the University, 138; position created, 135; position abolished, 183
Dean of Women, 135, 139
Denbo, Bruce F., 184
Dentistry, College of, 178, 193, 197
Dickey, Frank G., 164, 177, 196-97; named as President, 195
Dimock, William W., 52, 106
Director of Libraries, 167
Discipline Committee, 64, 78
Distinguished Professor, rank of, 165
Distinguished Professor of the Year, 138, 166
Dixon, Frank, 16
Donovan, Herman L., 138-39, 143-45, 148-54, 156-59, 163-66, 169-70, 172, 176-78, 187-92, 194-96; named as President, 133-34; President of Southern Association of Colleges and Secondary Schools, 134; favors liberal education, 137; inauguration of, 139-40; offered presidency of Peabody College, 146; urges faculty participation in policy making, 146-47; Vice President of

Donovan, H. L. (*continued*):
National Association of State Universities, 183
Donovan Hall, 187
Dormitories, 58, 84-85
Downing, Harold H., 132
Dummit, Eldon S., 191

Eastern Kentucky State College, 50, 91, 133-34
Eaton, Clement, 166, 182
Economics, Department of, 71, 112
Economics and Sociology, Department of, 58, 70
Education, College of, 69, 71, 73, 83, 88, 101, 111, 128, 133, 146, 164-65, 181, 195
Education, Department of, 68-69, 83
Education, School of, 3, 6, 15, 42-43
Education Building, 3, 83, 87
Educational Administration and Supervision, Department of, 69
Educational Commission, 68, 92
Educational Psychology, Department of, 69
Edwards, Philip R., 165
Ellis, G. W., 67
Ellis Bill, 68
Engineering, College of, 5, 60-61, 76, 86, 95, 105, 116, 119, 123, 133, 140-42, 157, 164, 176, 181, 184
Engineering Annexes, 116-17
Engineering Building, 163-64
Engineers Specialist School, 141
England, Merton, 166
English, Department of, 6, 76, 81, 132, 138, 165, 181, 182
English, Speech, and Dramatic Arts, Department of, 181
Enlisted Reserve Corps, 51, 140
Entomology, Department of, 6
Erikson, Statie, 88, 118
Eubanks, Charles L., 174-75
Evans, Alvin, 72
Experiment Station, *see* Agricultural Experiment Station

Fairfax, John C., 23
Farm and Home Week, 61, 73, 104

Farm Economics, Department of, 181
Farquhar, E. F., 132
Farris, Elgan, 139
Fayette County Medical Society, 193
Fergus, E. N., 142
Fields, William J., 70, 74
Fine Arts Building, 120, 162, 186, 188
Finley, John H., 85
Flag rush, 19
Football, 12-13, 79, 98, 113-14, 129-30, 150, 170-71, 180
Ford, H. Church, 175
Founders Day, 148
Founders Week, 186
Fox, John, Jr., 16
Franklin, Esther Cole, 102
Fraternities, 13-14, 79
Frazee, David H., 87
Frazee Hall, 3, 87
Freeman, W. E., 103
Funkhouser, William D., 54, 65, 72, 77, 90, 105, 125, 132, 164, 167; becomes Head of Department of Zoology, 52; Fellow of Entomological Society of America, 56; named as Dean of Graduate School, 70

Gamage, Harry, 98-99, 113
Gatton, Harper, 195
General Education Board, 30, 83
Geography, Department of, 139
Geological Museum, 90
Geology, Department of, 6, 126-27
German, Department of, 112, 132, 181
Gillis, Ezra L, 40; President of American Association of College Registrars, 56; starts institute for training registrars, 73
Ginger, Lyman, 183-84
Good, E. S., 106, 132
Governing Relations of the University, 147
Governor of Kentucky, ex officio member of Board of Trustees, 60
Graduate Faculty, 105
Graduate School, 5, 70, 87, 100, 175

Graduate School Committee, 58-60, 87

Graham, James H., 103-104, 115-16, 119, 122-23, 157-58, 164; named as Dean of College of Engineering, 104

Greek, Department of, 6

Grehan, Enoch, 11, 186

Guignol Theater, 96, 162, 186

Gymnasium, 3, 77

Haggin, James Ben Ali, 126

Haggin, Margaret Voorhies, 126

Haggin Fund, 126, 128, 144-45, 151, 166

Haggin Hall, 197

Haggin Publications Committee, 142

Hall, Ellery, 132

Hammonds, Carsie, 70

Hankins, Thomas L., 173

Hartford, Ellis, 139

Hatch, John Wesley, 175

Haun, Robert D., 132

Hazing, 21-22, 63, 79

Headley, Hal Price, 155

Health and Hygiene, Department of, 3, 53-54, 58, 120, 189

Heating plant, need for, 86

Highway Research Laboratory, 146

Hill, Henry H., 138

Hill-Burton Act, 190

History, Department of, 6, 87, 125, 132, 182, 185

History and Philosophy of Education, Department of, 69

History Club, 15

Hobson, Robert, 195

Holmes, Sarah B., 139

Holmes Hall, 187, 197

Home Economics, Department of, 3, 55, 86, 88

Home Economics, School of, 6

Home Economics Building, 118

Home economics education, 69

Home Economics Education, Department of, 33

Home Economics Extension, 92

Honorary fraternities, 79

Honors Day, 148

Hopkins, James F., 185

Horace Mann Literary Society, 15

Horine, John S., 132-33

Horticulture and Botany, Department of, 6

Hughes, Raymond M., report, 123-24

Huguelet, Guy, 167

Hurley, Patrick J., 83

Hygiene and Public Health, Department of, 3, 53-54, 58, 120, 189

Industrial education, 69

Industrial Education, Department of, 173

Investigating Committee of 1917, 38-39, 42-45, 49, 54, 59-60, 65

Jewell, Frances, 54, 72

Jewell Hall, 118

John, Fritz, 102

Johnson, Clyde, 150

Johnson, Keen, 135

Johnson, Lyman T., 175-76

Jones, J. Catron, 52, 101

Jones, T. T., 103, 165

Journal of Farm Economics, 185

Journal of Southern History, 166, 185

Journalism, Department of, 76, 82, 96, 112, 124, 181

Journalism, School of, 11, 181

Journalism Building, 163, 186

Kampus Kat, 97

Kastle, Joseph H., 4, 25, 29, 35-36

Kastle Hall, 3, 76, 120

Kavanaugh, George, 183

Keeneland Foundation, 144, 145, 151, 155, 166, 187

Keeneland Hall, 187

Kelly, John Sims, 98-99

Kentuckian, 17, 46

Kentucky Court of Appeals, 1, 116, 127-28, 145, 151, 157, 167-68

Kentucky Department of Agriculture, 24-25

Kentucky Department of Finance, 153

Kentucky Division of Personnel, 153, 155

Kentucky Education Association, 91-92, 107
Kentucky Farm Bureau, 156
Kentucky General Assembly, 27, 31, 33, 67, 75, 78, 80, 143, 148, 154, 174
Kentucky Geological Survey, 186
Kentucky High School Quarterly, 17
Kentucky Kernel, 16, 91, 99, 113, 115-16, 121, 131, 135
Kentucky Law Journal, 16, 185
Kentucky Medical Sciences Development Foundation, 193
Kentucky Mining Society, 14
Kentucky Press Association, 50
Kentucky Research Foundation, 142, 166
Kentucky State Auditor, report of, 31
Kentucky State Board of Agriculture, 37, 60
Kentucky State College, 174-75
Kentucky State Highway Commission, 105
Kentucky State Medical Association, 192
Kentucky 31 fescue, 187
Kentucky Trotting Horse Breeders' Association, 51
Kentucky University, 162
Kernel Press, 82
Kerr, Charles, 28
King, Margaret I., 73, 167
Kinkead, W. B., 85
Kinkead Hall, 162
Kirwan, A. D., 129, 150, 164-65, 177, 183
Kiwanis clubs, 90-91
Knight, Grant C., 52, 138, 165
Koppius, Otto T., 132
Kuiper, John, 195

Lafferty, William T., 1, 71
Lafferty Hall, 117
Laffoon, Ruby, 92
Lampert, Carl A., 52
Latin, Department of, 6
Law, College of, 1, 4, 6, 28, 30, 71-72, 133, 164, 175, 181, 195
Law Building, 116-17

Legislative Research Commission, 192-93
LeStourgeon, Flora E., 52
Library, 4, 85; growth of, 28-29, 57, 73, 89, 127, 185
Library science, 105
Library Science, Department of, 138
Ligon, Moses E., 69
Literary Club, 15
Literature, Philosophy, and the Arts, Division of, 138
Logan, M. M., 95
Louisville and Nashville Railroad, 25
Louisville *Courier-Journal*, 67, 155-56, 191
Louisville *Evening Post*, 67
Lukeman, Augustus, 110
Lunde, Robert G., 132

McCreary, James B., 27
McFarlan, Arthur C., 52-53, 166
McFarland, Frank T., 52
McHargue, J. S., 107
McIntyre, R. D., 132
Mackenzie, Alexander St. Clair, 5, 14, 28-29, 70
McVey, Frances, 90, 108, 118, 131-32
McVey, Frank L., 48-49, 51-61, 63, 65, 80, 85-88, 90-98, 100-108, 112-16, 120-27, 133, 135, 143, 148, 152, 159, 170, 189-90, 196; inauguration of, 50; strengthens faculty, 52-53; President of American Association for Agricultural Legislation, 55-56; President of National Association of State Universities, 56; surveys higher education in Oklahoma, 56; defends University's teaching of evolution, 67; recommends establishment of College of Education, 69; recommends establishment of College of Commerce, 70; second marriage of, 72; estimates future enrollment, 75; lists building needs, 75-76; President of Kentucky Education Association, 107; President of Association of Land Grant Colleges and

McVey, F. L. (continued):
Universities, 107; President of Southern Association of Colleges and Secondary Schools, 107; retirement of, 130-32; definition of a university, 131-32; death of, 185
McVey Hall, 81-82, 86, 120, 186
Maintenance and Operations, Department of, 139, 162, 186
Margaret I. King Library, 185
Markets and Rural Finance, Department of, 181
Martin, J. Holmes, 132
Martin, James W., 88, 165
Massie, Francis, 193
Mathematics, Department of, 6, 71, 76, 81, 102, 132
Mauer, John, 100
Mawen Motor Corporation, 119
Maxson, Ralph N., 7, 102
Maxwell Place, 108
Mayo College, 172
Mechanical and Electrical Engineering, College of, 1, 4-5, 26, 30, 37, 44
Mechanical Engineering, Department of, 165
Mechanical Hall, 4, 41, 117
Medical Center, 178, 189, 197
Medical technology, 105
Medicine, College of, 100, 178, 194, 197
Melcher, C. R., 5, 95
Melton, James, 186
Memorial Building Fund, 77
Memorial Coliseum, 163, 186
Memorial Hall, 82-83, 118, 127
Men's Student Council, 78, 97, 99, 113
Meyer, A. J., 102, 119
Military Science, Department of, 6, 53, 86
Miller, Arthur M., 1, 46, 88
Miller Hall, 4, 127
Miner, James B., 52, 96
Mineral Industries Building, 186
Mines and Metallurgy, College of, 5-6, 37
Mining Engineering, College of, 1, 5, 27

Mining Engineering, Department of, 120
Mining Engineering Building, 4, 87, 127
Mining Laboratory, 186
Model High School, 5, 43, 54
Modern Foreign Languages, Department of, 181
Modern Languages, Department of, 6
Morehead State College, 91
Moreland, Roy, 133
Morgan, Thomas Hunt, 112
Morrill Act, 8
Morris, James E., 82
Mulligan house, 49
Mullins, E. Y., 67
Murray, Frank, 142
Murray State College, 91
Museum of Anthropology, 4
Music, Department of, 53, 58, 61, 76, 83, 162, 165, 186
Mutchler, Fred, 35-36, 52

National Collegiate Athletic Association, 179
Naval Training Unit, 51
Neff, Norman, 96
Nelson Tax Act, 74
Neville Hall, 4, 58, 120
Nichols, William E., 28
Noe, Cotton, 28, 69, 101
Northern Extension Center, 173-74, 184-85
Norwood, Charles J., 1, 27-28, 87
Norwood Hall, 87, 120, 162
Nursing, College of, 178, 193, 197

Oak Ridge Institute of Nuclear Studies, 166
Observatory, 4, 81
Omicron Delta Kappa, 79, 115
Oswald, John W., named as President, 197
Overstreet, Sam, 192

Pan-Hellenic Council, 14
Pardue, Louis A., 88, 132, 165, 168, 182, 195
Park, James, 12

Park, Russell Smith, 87
Patrick, Wellington, 69
Patterson, James Kennedy, 1-2, 7-11, 35, 39-40, 45, 110, 178; leaves property of, 64; death of, 64, 86
Patterson, Walter K., 2, 5, 110; death of, 86
Patterson Hall, 3, 33, 187
Patterson House, 86
Patterson Literary Society, 15
Peabody Education Fund, 30
Peak, David H., 134
Pence, Merry L., 56
Pence Hall, 4
Penrod, E. B., 165
Personnel Bureau, 79
Peter, Alfred M., 36
Peterson, Frank, 135, 183
Pharmacy, College of, 172, 176
Pharmacy Building, 197
Phi Alpha Delta, 14
Phi Beta Kappa, 14, 79
Philosophian Literary Society, 15
Philosophy, Department of, 6, 66, 88, 112
Physical Education, Department of, 6, 53, 112, 129, 162
Physical Sciences, Division of, 138
Physics, Department of, 6, 71, 88, 112, 120, 132
Physics-Chemistry Building, 197
Plummer, Neil, 124
Police administration, 181
Poling, Daniel E., 186
Political Economy Club, 15
Political Science, Department of, 72, 101, 112, 132
Practice High School, 5, 43, 54
Price, H. Bruce, 195
Princeton, Ky., 78
Provost, position created, 184
Pryor, Joseph W., 29, 56, 65, 88, 132
Psi Delta Phi, 14
Psychology, Department of, 53, 58, 61, 66, 71, 88, 96, 103, 120, 138
Public Works Administration, 115
Publicity and Alumni Affairs, Office of, 79
Purnell Act, 74

Quarter system, 145
Queen and Crescent Railway, 41
Quicksand, Ky., 78
Quill, Laurence L., 169

Racial integration, 174-76
Radio listening centers, 105, 137
Rankin, Fred, 190
Rannells, Edward, 88
Rash, J. R., 67
Rash bill, 68
Reeves, Floyd W., 70
Reorganization Act of 1934, 143
Research and publication, 166, 184-85
Research Club, 56
Reserve Officer Training Corps, 23, 51, 53-54, 140
Rhoads, McHenry, 43, 70
Richmond, James H., 92
Riley, Herbert L., 139
Roberts, George, 36
Roberts, William L., 52
Robinson Foundation, 78
Rockefeller Foundation, 102
Romance Languages, Department of, 112, 138, 181
Romany Theater, 76, 96
Rose, Wickliffe, 30
Ross, Clay C., 70, 142
Rowe, Walter E., 1, 27, 37-38, 45
Rupp, Adolph, 100, 150, 178
Rural Church Institutes, 104
Rural Sociology, 185
Rural Sociology, Department of, 181
Russell, John Dale, 70

Sanders, Irwin, 182
Sayre School, 161
Scherago, Morris, 52, 182
Schwendeman, Joseph R., 139
Science, School of, 6
Science Hall, 4
Scopes trial, 66
Scovell, Melville A., 1, 3-4, 7, 30, 33, 51
Scovell Park, 83
Seaton, Don Cash, 165
Seay, Maurice, 142, 165, 183
Semple, Ellen, 89

Service Building, 186
Shannon, Jasper B., 102, 132
Shaver, Robert E., 165, 195
Shawneetown, 161, 187
Shively, Bernie, 129, 171
Sigma Xi, 14, 56
Simrall, Josephine, 54
Sloan Foundation, 126
Slone, Earl J., 172
Small-Animal House, 81
Smith-Hughes Act, 33, 50, 55
Smith-Lever Act, 26, 32-35
Snow, Louis F., 1-2
Social organizations, 79
Social Studies, Division of, 138
Social Work, Department of, 139
Sociology, Department of, 112, 181, 184
Soil Physics, Department of, 6
Sororities, 13-14, 79
South, Dudley, 132
Southeastern Conference, 99-100, 179
Southern Association of Colleges and Secondary Schools, 154
Southern Conference, 90
Southern Railroad, 24-25
Southern Regional Education Program, 188-89
Spindletop Farm, 152
Spivey, Herman E., 165, 181-82
Sprowles, Lee, 165
Stadium, 77-78
Stahr, Elvis, 112, 164, 177, 195; named as Provost, 184
Staples, Charles R., 89
State Board of Education, 92
State Budget Commission, 111
State Building Commission, 153
State Department of Education, 155
State University, Lexington, Ky., 1, 2, 7, 10-11
Stein, Edwin, 165
Stoll, Richard C., 28, 93, 130, 133, 167, 176
Stoll Field, 77, 121
Streit, Saul, 179
Strollers, 15, 66, 97
Student government, 17-19, 43, 64, 128-29, 135-36

Student Union Building, 86, 115-16, 122, 135
Students, Barker's attitude toward, 11, 13, 17-18
Students' Army Training Corps, 51
Sullivan, Rodman, 132
Sulzer, Elmer, 105
Superintendent of Public Instruction, 60, 92
Survey Commission of 1917, 38-40, 43-45, 49, 57, 60, 65, 68
Sweetland, Edwin R., 28

Tau Beta Kake, 15-16
Tau Beta Pi, 14
Tau Kappa Alpha, 14
Taylor, William S., 69, 88, 164
Taylor, Zachary, papers presented to library, 185
Teachers College, 1, 3, 5
Tennessee Valley Authority, 106
Terrell, Daniel V., 164, 183
Terrell, Glanville, 7, 88-89
Thompson, Lawrence S., 167, 182
Tigert, John J., 18, 56
Tobacco research, 141-42
Tobacco Research Laboratory, 116
Townsend, William H., 28
Training School Building, 83, 87
Transit, 16
Transylvania College, 195
Trout, Allen M., 155
Tug of war, 20, 63
Turck, Charles J., 71-72, 90-91
Tuthill, James Edward, 7
Tuttle, Franklin E., 7

Union Literary Society, 15
United States Armed Forces Institute, 141
University Assembly, 2, 60, 94
University Book Store, 77
University College, 149-50
University Commons, 81, 120
University Council, 2, 40, 50, 59-60
University Elementary School, 83
University Extension, Department of, 54-55, 73, 173
University Faculty, 2, 7, 9, 21, 40-41, 135, 147-50, 184, 191, 193

University High School, 69-70, 83
University Hospital, 197
University of Kentucky, service to
state, 24; enrollment, 29, 66, 75,
81, 95, 128, 146, 160, 185; investigation of, 37-47; faculty and
staff, 43-44, 62, 93-94, 125, 164,
168, 180-81; role in wartime, 50-
51, 140-41; accreditation, 57, 65;
compared with other universities,
61-62; financial support, 62, 74-
75, 81, 93-94, 109-10, 143, 145-46,
160-61, 185; building program, 76,
81, 161-62; awards first Ph.D., 87;
operates radio station, 137; influx
of veterans, 160; aids University
of Indonesia, 182
University of Louisville, 189-92
University Personnel Service, 96
University Post Office, 77, 82
University Press, 106, 126, 135, 142,
162, 184-86
University Senate, 59-60, 64, 71, 78,
87, 111, 125, 128, 130, 135-36, 146
University Training School, 139, 164

Valleau, William D., 52, 106, 165
Vandenbosch, Amry, 102, 132, 165,
182
Viking Foundation, 119-20
Vocational Education, Department
of, 33
Vocational Teacher Training, 69

Wall, Willem van de, 105
War Memorial Building, 76
Ward, William S., 182

Watkins, J. Stephen, 185, 193
Webb, William S., 72, 90, 106, 127,
132, 142
Welch, Frank J., 156, 195
Wendt, Henry W., 76
Wenner-Gren, Axel, 119, 157-58
Wenner-Gren Aeronautical Research
Laboratory, 157-58
Wesley, William C., 173
Western Kentucky State College, 50,
91, 134, 189-90
Wetherby, Lawrence, 155
Wetzel, Harold, 139
White, James G., 2, 5, 19
White, Martin M., 88, 149, 164
White Hall, 4, 58, 70, 120
White Mathematics Club, 15
Whitehead, Don, 186
Wiest, Edward, 52, 65, 70
Willard, William R., 194
Williams, J. D., 139
Willis, Simeon, 145, 148
Wilson, Samuel M., 28, 167
Women's Administration Council,
78
Women's Building, 86
Woods, Ralph H., 70
Wootton, Bailey P., 95
World War I, 50-51
World War II, 137-51
Wynne, C. A., 113-14, 129

Yates, James Anderson, 87
YMCA, 15, 50, 61

Zoology, Department of, 6, 53, 112,
118, 132

THIS BOOK has been published by the University of Kentucky Press as a part of the celebration of the University's Centennial, 1965. Its author, who holds three degrees from the University, is associate professor of history at the Northern Community College, Covington. The book is designed by P. J. Conkwright, also an alumnus of the University, which has awarded him the Litt.D. degree in recognition of his outstanding work as typographer for Princeton University Press.